THE ULTIMATE

NINJA

Speedi

COOKBOOK

FOR BEGINNERS

1200

Days Easy and Tasty Ninja
Speedi Recipes with 14-Day
Meal Plan to Air Fry, Bake,
Roast, Dehydrate, Slow Cook
and More for Beginners

BERTHA BILES

Table of Content

INTRODUCTION

I had always been a bit intimidated by pressure cookers. The idea of all that steam and hissing made me nervous. But then, one day, I was browsing through a kitchen store and I saw the Ninja Speedi Rapid Cooker & Air Fryer. It looked different than other pressure cookers I had seen before - more sleek and modern, with an air fryer built in too. I was intrigued.

I started reading up on the Ninja Speedi and was impressed by all its features. It promised to cook meals up to 70% faster than traditional methods, and could be used for everything from soups and stews to desserts and even air frying. I decided to take the plunge and bought one.

At first, I was a bit hesitant to use it. But once I got the hang of it, I was hooked. The Ninja Speedi made cooking so much faster and easier, and the food always turned out delicious. I started experimenting with different recipes and soon had a whole collection of favorites.

I'm so glad I decided to try it out - it's become an indispensable tool in my kitchen!

I collected some of my go-to recipes for the Ninja Speedi Rapid Cooker and Air Fryer, and want to share with my readers now.

This cookbook just a few examples, but I've found that the Ninja Speedi is incredibly versatile and can be used for a wide range of recipes.

CHAPTER 1:
NINJA SPEEDI RAPDI COOKER & AIR FRYER 101

The Overview of Ninja Speedi Rapid Cooker & Air Fryer

The Ninja Speedi Rapid Cooker is a versatile kitchen appliance that combines the functions of Rapid Cooker and Air Fry/Stovetop all in one. In the Rapid Cooker Mode, you can use Speedi Meals, Steam & Crisp, Steam & Bake, Steam and Proof functions. In the Air Fry/Stovetop Mode, you can use Air Fry, Bake/Roast, Broil, Dehydrate, Sear/Sauté, Slow Cook and Sous Vide functions. All of them are designed to save time and effort in the kitchen, allowing you to cook meals quickly and easily without sacrificing flavor.

With its advanced heating technology, the Ninja Speedi Rapid Cooker can cook food up to 70% faster than traditional cooking methods, making it ideal for busy families and individuals who want to eat healthy meals without spending hours in the kitchen. It also features a large cooking capacity, allowing you to cook multiple servings at once.

Overall, the Ninja Speedi Rapid Cooker is a convenient and efficient appliance that can help you prepare delicious and healthy meals in no time.

Advantages of Ninja Speedi Rapid Cooker & Air Fryer

Ninja Speedi Rapid Cooker & Air Fryer has lots of advantages because of its 12 functions, here is listed 6 advantages as I known.

Versatility: The Ninja Speedi offers 12 different cooking functions, including air fry, roast, bake, broil, and more, making it a versatile kitchen appliance for a variety of cooking needs.

Time-saving: The rapid cooker function allows for faster cooking times, reducing the amount of time needed to cook meals compared to traditional cooking methods.

Healthier cooking: The air fry function allows for healthier cooking with little to no oil, resulting in crispy and delicious food without the added calories and fat.

Easy to use: The Ninja Speedi is designed with user-friendly controls and a digital display for easy operation, making it accessible for cooks of all levels.

Large capacity: With a 6.5-quart cooking pot, the Ninja Speedi can accommodate large meals, making it ideal for families or entertaining.

Easy to clean: The non-stick cooking pot and accessories are dishwasher safe, making cleaning up after cooking a breeze.

Tips and Tricks to Make Most of Ninja Speedi

Speedi Meals: This function is perfect for when you want to cook something quickly. I like to use it to make rice, pasta, and other grains. It's also great for cooking vegetables and fish.

Steam and Crisp: This function is perfect for cooking vegetables and meats. It steams the food first and then crisps it up for a delicious texture.

Steam and Bake: This function is great for making baked goods, like cakes and bread. The steam helps to keep the food moist and fluffy.

Steam: This function is perfect for cooking vegetables and fish. It helps to retain the nutrients and flavor of the food.

Proof: This function is great for proofing bread and other baked goods. It creates the perfect environment for the dough to rise.

Air Fry: This function is perfect for making crispy and delicious foods, like french fries and chicken wings. It's a healthier alternative to deep frying.

Bake/Roast: This function is great for baking and roasting meats, vegetables, and fruits. It creates a crispy exterior and a juicy interior.

Broil: This function is perfect for cooking meats and vegetables quickly. It creates a delicious charred exterior.

Dehydrate: This function is great for making dried fruits, jerky, and other snacks. It's a great way to preserve food and create healthy snacks.

Sear/Sauté: This function is perfect for cooking meats and vegetables quickly. It creates a delicious sear on the exterior of the food.

Slow Cook: This function is great for making stews, soups, and other slow-cooked dishes. It's a great way to infuse flavors and create tender meats.

Sous Vide: This function is perfect for cooking meats and vegetables at a low temperature for a long time. It creates perfectly cooked and tender food.

How to Use Ninja Speedi Rapid Cooker?

Using the SmartSwitch

The SmartSwitch allows you to select between the Rapid Cooker mode and Air Fry/Stovetop mode. The SmartSwitch's position will determine which cooking functions are available for selection.

When you select the Rapid Cooker by keeping the handle pointing upwards, this unlocks the following cooking function on the appliance:

* Speedi Meals   *Steam and Crisp

* Steam and Bake   *Steam   *Proof

Then you can turn the Smart Switch to the downward position, and you can then unlock the other cooking options like:

* Air Fry   * Bake/Roast   * Sear/Sauté   * Slow Cook

Sous Vide   * Broil   * Dehydrate

Set Up a Rapid Cooker Recipe

* Place the Crisper Tray in the bottom position in the pot, then place ingredients on the tray. To use the Crisper Tray in the bottom position, push in the legs, then place the tray in the pot.

* Close the lid and flip the SmartSwitch down. Only Air Fry/Stovetop functions will illuminate when switch is in downward position.

* Set the temp and time. Press START/STOP to begin cooking. (When using Air Fry and Bake & Roast functions, be sure to add an additional 5 minutes to your total cook time to allow for preheat. Add ingredients after the first 5 minutes.)

* When cook time reaches zero, the unit will beep and "End".

Set Up a Rapid Cooker Recipe

* Add liquid to the bottom of the pot per recipe instructions.

* Place the Crisper Tray in the elevated position in the pot, then place ingredients on the tray. To use the Crisper Tray in the elevated position, pull out the legs, then place the tray in the pot.

* Close the lid and flip the SmartSwitch up. Use the center arrows to select a function. Only Rapid Cooker functions will illuminate when switch is in upward position.

* Set the temp and time. Press START/STOP to begin cooking. Progress bars indicate unit is building steam. When unit switches to convection cooking, timer will start counting down.

Speedi Meals 101

Speedi Meals is the special cooking function for busy people, it can cook one meal all in one pot within 30 minutes. Here is a simple guide for you to use this function.

Crisper Tray Layer (Protein): Pick your favorite protein and season as desired. Place the Crisper Tray in the elevated position to create the perfect airflow.

Bottom Layer (Grains & Pasta): Choose from a variety of grains or pasta. Add the desired amount to the bottom of the pot.

Directions:

1. **Pour in the grain or pasta**. Start by pouring your grain or pasta into the bottom of the pot.

2. **Add liquid**. Now that your ingredients are in the bottom of the pot, add water, stock, or sauce and stir until combined.

3. **Prep and season protein**. Prepare your desired protein, then place protein on the Crisper Tray in the elevated position and close the lid.

4. **Cook**. Flip the SmartSwitch up to Rapid Cooker mode and select Speedi Meals. Set temp and time based on protein.

1. Pour in the grain or pasta

2. Add liquid

3.Prep and season protein

4. Cook

How to Clean the Ninja Speedi Rapid Cooker & Air Fryer?

Here are some tips and steps on how to clean your Ninja Speedi Rapid Cooker and Air Fryer:

Unplug the appliance and allow it to cool down before cleaning.

* Remove any excess food or grease from the cooking basket or pot with a paper towel or a soft-bristled brush.

* If the cooking basket or pot is dishwasher safe, you can place it in the dishwasher. Otherwise, hand wash it with warm soapy water and a non-abrasive sponge or cloth. Do not use steel wool or abrasive cleaners as they can scratch the surface.

* To clean the inside of the appliance, use a damp cloth or sponge and wipe it down thoroughly. Do not immerse the appliance in water or any other liquid.

* If there are any stubborn stains or residue, you can use a non-abrasive cleaner and a soft-bristled brush to gently scrub it off.

* To clean the exterior of the appliance, use a damp cloth or sponge and wipe it down. Do not use abrasive cleaners or harsh chemicals.

* For the control panel, use a damp cloth or sponge to wipe it down. Do not use abrasive cleaners or submerge the control panel in water.

* After cleaning, allow all parts to dry completely before reassembling the appliance.

By following these tips and steps, you can ensure that your Ninja Speedi Rapid Cooker and Air Fryer is clean and ready to use for your next meal.

BASIC KITCHEN CONVERSIONS & EQUIVALENTS

DRY MEASUREMENTS CONVERSION CHART

3 teaspoons = 1 tablespoon = 1/16 cup
6 teaspoons = 2 tablespoons = 1/8 cup
12 teaspoons = 4 tablespoons = ¼ cup
24 teaspoons = 8 tablespoons = ½ cup
36 teaspoons = 12 tablespoons = ¾ cup
48 teaspoons = 16 tablespoons = 1 cup

METRIC TO US COOKING CONVERSIONS

OVEN TEMPERATURES

120 °C = 250 °F
160 °C = 320 °F
180 °C = 350 °F
205 °C = 400 °F
220 °C = 425 °F

LIQUID MEASUREMENTS CONVERSION CHART

8 fluid ounces = 1 cup = ½ pint = ¼ quart
16 fluid ounces = 2 cups = 1 pint = ½ quart
32 fluid ounces = 4 cups = 2 pints = 1 quart = ¼ gallon
128 fluid ounces = 16 cups = 8 pints = 4 quarts = 1 gallon

BAKING IN GRAMS

1 cup flour = 140 grams
1 cup sugar = 150 grams
1 cup powdered sugar = 160 grams
1 cup heavy cream = 235 grams

VOLUME

1 milliliter = 1/5 teaspoon
5 ml = 1 teaspoon
15 ml = 1 tablespoon
240 ml = 1 cup or 8 fluid ounces
1 liter = 34 fluid ounces

WEIGHT

1 gram = .035 ounces
100 grams = 3.5 ounces
500 grams = 1.1 pounds
1 kilogram = 35 ounces

US TO METRIC COOKING CONVERSIONS

1/5 tsp = 1 ml
1 tsp = 5 ml
1 tbsp = 15 ml
1 fluid ounces = 30 ml
1 cup = 237 ml
1 pint (2 cups) = 473 ml
1 quart (4 cups) = .95 liter
1 gallon (16 cups) = 3.8 liters
1 oz = 28 grams
1 pound = 454 grams

BUTTER

1 cup butter = 2 sticks = 8 ounces = 230 grams = 16 tablespoons
WHAT DOES 1 CUP EQUAL
1 cup = 8 fluid ounces
1 cup = 16 tablespoons
1 cup = 48 teaspoons
1 cup = ½ pint
1 cup = ¼ quart
1 cup = 1/16 gallon
1 cup = 240 ml

BAKING PAN CONVERSIONS

9-inch round cake pan = 12 cups
10-inch tube pan =16 cups
10-inch bundt pan = 12 cups
9-inch springform pan = 10 cups
9 x 5 inch loaf pan = 8 cups
inch square pan = 8 cups

BAKING PAN CONVERSIONS

1 cup all-purpose flour = 4.5 oz
1 cup rolled oats = 3 oz
1 large egg = 1.7 oz
1 cup butter = 8 oz
1 cup milk = 8 oz
1 cup heavy cream = 8.4 oz
1 cup granulated sugar = 7.1 oz
1 cup packed brown sugar = 7.75 oz
1 cup vegetable oil = 7.7 oz
1 cup unsifted powdered sugar = 4.4 oz

CHAPTER 2:
BREAKFAST RECIPES

Toasties and Sausage in Egg Pond (Steam&Crisp)

Prep: 10 minutes, Total Cook Time: 26 minutes, Steam: approx. 4 minutes, Cook: 22 minutes, Serves: 2

3 eggs   2 cooked sausages, sliced
1 bread slice, cut into sticks
⅛ cup mozzarella cheese, grated

⅛ cup Parmesan cheese, grated
¼ cup cream   Cooking spray

1. Pour 1 cup water into the pot. Push in the legs on the Crisper Tray, then place the tray in the bottom position in the pot. Spray 2 ramekins with cooking spray.
2. Whisk together eggs with cream in a bowl and place in the ramekins.
3. Stir in the bread and sausage slices in the egg mixture and top with cheese.
4. Transfer the ramekins on the tray.
5. Close the lid and flip the SmartSwitch to Rapid Cooker. Select STEAM & CRISP, set temperature to 365°F, and set time to 22 minutes. Press START/STOP to begin cooking (the unit will steam for approx. 4 minutes before crisping).
6. When cooking is complete, serve warm.

Zucchini Fritters (Steam&Crisp)

Prep: 15 minutes, Total Cook Time: 14 minutes, Steam: approx. 4 minutes, Cook: 10 minutes, Serves: 4

½ cup water, for steaming
7 ounces Halloumi cheese
2 eggs
Salt and black pepper, to taste

10½ ounces zucchini, grated and squeezed
¼ cup all-purpose flour
1 tsp. fresh dill, minced

1. Pour ½ cup water into the pot. Push in the legs on the Crisper Tray, then place the tray in the bottom position in the pot.
2. Mix together all the ingredients in a large bowl.
3. Make small fritters from this mixture and place them on the tray.
4. Close the lid and flip the SmartSwitch to Rapid Cooker. Select STEAM & CRISP, set temperature to 360°F, and set time to 10 minutes. Press START/STOP to begin cooking (the unit will steam for approx. 4 minutes before crisping).
5. With 5 minutes remaining, open the lid and toss the fritters with tongs. Close the lid to continue cooking.
6. When cooking is complete, use tongs to remove the fritters from the tray and serve warm.

Egg Veggie Frittata (Steam&Bake)

Prep: 10 minutes, Total Cook Time: 35 minutes, Steam: approx. 20 minutes, Cook: 15 minutes, Serves: 2

1 cup water, for steaming

½ cup milk

¼ cup baby Bella mushrooms, chopped

¼ cup spinach, chopped

½ tsp. salt

Dash of hot sauce

4 eggs

2 green onions, chopped

1 tbsp. butter

½ tsp. black pepper

1. Pour 1 cup water into the pot. Push in the legs on the Crisper Tray, then place the tray in the bottom position in the pot. Grease 6x3 inch square pan with butter.
2. Whisk eggs with milk in a large bowl and stir in green onions, mushrooms and spinach.
3. Sprinkle with salt, black pepper and hot sauce and pour this mixture into the prepared pan. Then place the pan on the tray.
4. Close the lid and flip the SmartSwitch to Rapid Cooker. Select STEAM & BAKE, set temperature to 350°F, and set time to 15 minutes. Press START/STOP to begin cooking (the unit will steam for approx. 20 minutes before baking).
5. Dish out in a platter and serve warm.

Flavorful Bacon Cups (Steam&Bake)

Prep: 10 minutes, Total Cook Time: 35 minutes, Steam: approx. 20 minutes, Cook: 15 minutes, Serves: 6

1 cup water, for steaming

6 bread slices

3 tbsps. green bell pepper, seeded and chopped

6 bacon slices

1 scallion, chopped

6 eggs

Cooking spray

2 tbsps. low-fat mayonnaise

1. Pour 1 cup water into the pot. Push in the legs on the Crisper Tray, then place the tray in the bottom position in the pot. Spray 6 cups muffin tin with cooking spray.
2. Place each bacon slice in a prepared muffin cup.
3. Cut the bread slices with round cookie cutter and place over the bacon slices.
4. Top with bell pepper, scallion and mayonnaise evenly and crack 1 egg in each muffin cup. Then place the muffin cups on the tray.
5. Close the lid and flip the SmartSwitch to Rapid Cooker. Select STEAM & BAKE, set temperature to 350°F, and set time to 15 minutes. Press START/STOP to begin cooking (the unit will steam for approx. 20 minutes before baking).
6. Dish out and serve warm.

Parmesan Sausage Egg Muffins (Steam&Bake)

Prep: 5 minutes, Total Cook Time: 35 minutes, Steam: approx. 20 minutes, Cook: 15 minutes, Serves: 4

1 cup water, for steaming   cooking spray
6 ounces (170 g) Italian sausage, sliced
6 eggs   ⅛ cup heavy cream
Salt and ground black pepper, to taste
3 ounces (85 g) Parmesan cheese, grated

1. Pour 1 cup water into the pot. Push in the legs on the Crisper Tray, then place the tray in the bottom position in the pot. Spray a muffin pan with cooking spray.
2. Put the sliced sausage in the muffin pan. Beat the eggs with the cream in a bowl and season with salt and pepper. Pour half of the mixture over the sausages in the pan. Sprinkle with cheese and the remaining egg mixture. Then place the pan on the tray.
3. Close the lid and flip the SmartSwitch to Rapid Cooker. Select STEAM & BAKE, set temperature to 350°F, and set time to 15 minutes. Press START/STOP to begin cooking (the unit will steam for approx. 20 minutes before baking).
4. When cooking is complete, serve immediately.

Cream Bread (Steam&Bake)

Prep: 20 minutes, Total Cook Time: 55 minutes, Steam: approx. 25 minutes, Cook: 30 minutes, Serves: 12

2 cups water, for steaming   cooking spray   2 tbsps. milk powder   ¾ cup whipping cream
1 cup milk   1 large egg   1 tsp. salt   ¼ cup fine sugar
4½ cups bread flour   ½ cup all-purpose flour   3 tsps. dry yeast

1. Pour 2 cups water into the pot. Push in the legs on the Crisper Tray, then place the
2.   tray in the bottom position in the pot. Spray 2 loaf pans with cooking spray.
3. Mix together all the dry ingredients with the wet ingredients to form a dough.
4. Divide the dough into 4 equal-sized balls and roll each ball into a rectangle.
5. Roll each rectangle like a Swiss roll tightly and place 2 rolls into each prepared loaf pan.
6. Keep aside for about 1 hour and place the loaf pans on the tray.
7. Close the lid and flip the SmartSwitch to Rapid Cooker. Select STEAM & BAKE, set temperature to 350°F, and set time to 30 minutes. Press START/STOP to begin cooking (the unit will steam for approx. 25 minutes before baking).
8. When cooking is complete, remove the bread rolls from pans
9. Cut each roll into desired size slices and serve warm.

Bacon and Hot Dogs Omelet (Steam&Bake)

Prep: 10 minutes, Total Cook Time: 30 minutes, Steam: approx. 20 minutes, Cook: 10 minutes, Serves: 2

1 cup water, for steaming	cooking spray	2 hot dogs, chopped	2 small onions, chopped
4 eggs	1 bacon slice, chopped	2 tbsps. milk	Salt and black pepper, to taste

1. Pour 1 cup water into the pot. Push in the legs on the Crisper Tray, then place the tray in the bottom position in the pot. Spray a 8-inch round baking pan with cooking spray.
2. Whisk together eggs and stir in the remaining ingredients.
3. Stir well to combine and place in the prepared pan, then place the pan on the tray.
4. Close the lid and flip the SmartSwitch to Rapid Cooker. Select STEAM & BAKE, set temperature to 325°F, and set time to 10 minutes. Press START/STOP to begin cooking (the unit will steam for approx. 20 minutes before baking).
5. When cooking is complete, serve hot.

Gold Avocado (Air Fry)

Prep Time: 5 minutes, Cook Time: 6 minutes, Serves: 4

cooking spray	2 large avocados, sliced
¼ tsp. paprika	Salt and ground black pepper, to taste
½ cup whole wheat flour	2 eggs, beaten
1 cup bread crumbs	

1. Push in the legs on the Crisper Tray, then place the tray in the bottom of the pot. Spray the tray with cooking spray.
2. Sprinkle paprika, salt and pepper on the slices of avocado.
3. Lightly coat the avocados with flour. Dredge them in the eggs, before covering with bread crumbs.
4. Close the lid and flip the SmartSwitch to AIRFRY/STOVETOP. Select AIRFRY, set temperature to 400°F, and set time to 11 minutes (unit will need to preheat for 5 minutes, so set an external timer if desired). Press START/STOP to begin cooking.
5. When the unit is preheated and the time reaches 6 minutes, place the avocados on the tray. Close the lid to begin cooking.
6. When cooking is complete, serve hot.

Simple Scotch Eggs (Bake&Roast)

Prep Time: 5 minutes, Cook Time: 25 minutes, Serves: 4

cooking spray   4 large hard boiled eggs   8 slices thick-cut bacon
1 (12-ounce / 340-g) package pork sausage

Special Equipment:

4 wooden toothpicks, soaked in water for at least 30 minutes

1. Slice the sausage into four parts and place each part into a large circle.
2. Put an egg into each circle and wrap it in the sausage. Put in the refrigerator for 1 hour.
3. Push in the legs on the Crisper Tray, then place the tray in the bottom of the pot. Spray the tray with cooking spray.
4. Make a cross with two pieces of thick-cut bacon. Put a wrapped egg in the center, fold the bacon over top of the egg, and secure with a toothpick.
5. Close the lid and flip the SmartSwitch to AIRFRY/STOVETOP. Select BAKE & ROAST, set temperature to 450°F, and set time to 30 minutes (unit will need to preheat for 5 minutes, so set an external timer if desired). Press START/STOP to begin cooking.
6. When the unit is preheated and the time reaches 25 minutes, place the eggs on the tray. Close the lid to begin cooking.
7. After 15 minutes, open the lid and flip the eggs with silicone-tipped tongs to ensure even cooking. Close the lid to continue cooking.
8. When cooking is complete, serve immediately.

Honey Carrot Cake Oatmeal (Slow Cook)

Prep Time: 12 minutes, Cook Time: 7 hours, Serves: 6

2 tbsps. melted coconut oil   4 cups water   2 cups almond milk
3 cups steel-cut oats   2 cups finely grated carrot   ¼ cup honey
1 (8-ounce / 227-g) BPA-free can unsweetened   2 tsps. vanilla extract   1 tsp. ground cinnamon
crushed pineapple in juice, undrained   ¼ tsp. salt

1. Before getting started, be sure to remove the crisper tray.
2. Grease the bottom of the pot with coconut oil.
3. Mix the steel-cut oats, carrot, and pineapple in the bottom of the pot.
4. Mix the almond milk, water, coconut oil, honey, vanilla, salt, and cinnamon in a medium bowl. Mix until combined well. Add this mixture into the pot.
5. Close the lid and flip the SmartSwitch to AIRFRY/STOVETOP. Select SLOW COOK, set temperature to "Lo", and set time to 7 hours. Press START/STOP to begin cooking, until the oatmeal is tender and the edges start to brown.
6. Enjoy!

Kale and Quinoa Egg Casserole (Slow Cook)

Prep Time: 13 minutes, Cook Time: 7 hours, Serves: 6 to 8

11 eggs 3 cups chopped kale
3 cups 2% milk
1½ cups quinoa, rinsed and drained
1½ cups vegetable broth

1½ cups shredded Havarti cheese
1 red bell pepper, stemmed, seeded, and chopped
1 leek, chopped 3 garlic cloves, minced

1. Before getting started, be sure to remove the crisper tray.
2. Grease the bottom of the pot lightly with vegetable oil and keep aside.
3. Mix the milk, vegetable broth, and eggs in a large bowl, and beat well with a wire whisk.
4. Stir in the kale, quinoa, leek, bell pepper, garlic, and cheese. Add this mixture into the pot.
5. Close the lid and flip the SmartSwitch to AIRFRY/STOVETOP. Select SLOW COOK, set temperature to "Lo", and set time to 7 hours. Press START/STOP to begin cooking, until a food thermometer registers 165ºF and the mixture is set.
6. Serve warm.

Tasty Toasts (Bake&Roast)

Prep Time: 10 minutes, Cook Time: 5 minutes, Serves: 4

cooking spray 4 bread slices
8 ounces ricotta cheese
4 ounces smoked salmon

1 shallot, sliced 1 cup arugula
1 garlic clove, minced 1 tsp. lemon zest
¼ tsp. freshly ground black pepper

1. Push in the legs on the Crisper Tray, then place the tray in the bottom of the pot. Spray the tray with cooking spray.
2. Close the lid and flip the SmartSwitch to AIRFRY/STOVETOP. Select BAKE & ROAST, set temperature to 350°F, and set time to 10 minutes (unit will need to preheat for 5 minutes, so set an external timer if desired). Press START/STOP to begin cooking.
3. When the unit is preheated and the time reaches 5 minutes, place the bread slices on the tray. Close the lid to begin cooking.
4. Put garlic, ricotta cheese and lemon zest in a food processor and pulse until smooth.
5. Spread this mixture over each bread slice and top with salmon, arugula and shallot.
6. Sprinkle with black pepper and serve warm.

CHAPTER 3:
VEGETABLES RECIPES

Herbed Potatoes (Steam&Crisp)

Prep: 20 minutes, Total Cook Time: 34 minutes, Steam: approx. 4 minutes, Cook: 30 minutes, Serves: 4

½ cup water, for steaming   6 small potatoes, chopped
2 tbsps. fresh parsley, chopped   3 tbsps. olive oil
2 tsps. mixed dried herbs
Salt and black pepper, to taste

1. Pour ½ cup water into the pot. Push in the legs on the Crisper Tray, then place the tray in the bottom position in the pot.
2. Mix the potatoes, oil, herbs, salt and black pepper in a bowl.
3. Arrange the chopped potatoes on the tray.
4. Close the lid and flip the SmartSwitch to Rapid Cooker. Select STEAM & CRISP, set temperature to 450°F, and set time to 30 minutes. Press START/ STOP to begin cooking (the unit will steam for approx. 4 minutes before crisping).
5. With 15 minutes remaining, open the lid and toss the potatoes with tongs. Close the lid to continue cooking.
6. When cooking is complete, use tongs to remove the potatoes from the tray. Serve garnished with parsley.

Sweet and Sour Brussels Sprouts (Steam&Crisp)

Prep: 10 minutes, Total Cook Time: 14 minutes, Steam: approx. 4 minutes, Cook: 10 minutes, Serves: 2

½ cup water, for steaming
2 cups Brussels sprouts, trimmed and halved lengthwise
1 tbsp. balsamic vinegar   1 tbsp. maple syrup
Salt, as required

1. Pour ½ cup water into the pot. Push in the legs on the Crisper Tray, then place the tray in the bottom position in the pot.
2. Mix all the ingredients in a bowl and toss to coat well. Arrange the Brussels sprouts on the tray.
3. Close the lid and flip the SmartSwitch to Rapid Cooker. Select STEAM & CRISP, set temperature to 400°F, and set time to 10 minutes. Press START/ STOP to begin cooking (the unit will steam for approx. 4 minutes before crisping).
4. With 5 minutes remaining, open the lid and toss the Brussels sprouts with tongs. Close the lid to continue cooking.
5. When cooking is complete, use tongs to remove the Brussels sprouts from the tray and serve hot.

Sweet and Spicy Parsnips (Steam&Crisp)

Prep: 15 minutes, Total Cook Time: 39 minutes, Steam: approx. 4 minutes, Cook: 35 minutes, Serves: 6

½ cup water, for steaming
2 pounds parsnip, peeled and cut into 1-inch chunks
1 tbsp. butter, melted   2 tbsps. honey
1 tbsp. dried parsley flakes, crushed
¼ tsp. red pepper flakes, crushed
Salt and ground black pepper, to taste

1. Pour ½ cup water into the pot. Push in the legs on the Crisper Tray, then place the tray in the bottom position in the pot.
2. Mix the parsnips and butter in a bowl and toss to coat well. Arrange the parsnip chunks on the tray.
3. Close the lid and flip the SmartSwitch to Rapid Cooker. Select STEAM & CRISP, set temperature to 400°F, and set time to 35 minutes. Press START/STOP to begin cooking (the unit will steam for approx. 4 minutes before crisping).
4. With 15 minutes remaining, open the lid and flip the parsnip chunks with tongs. Close the lid to continue cooking.
5. With 5 minutes remaining, open the lid. Mix the remaining ingredients in another large bowl and stir in the parsnip chunks. Transfer the parsnip chunks to the tray. Close the lid to continue cooking.
6. Dish out the parsnip chunks onto serving plates and serve hot.

Balsamic-Glazed Vegetables and Couscous (Slow Cook)

Prep Time: 15 minutes, Cook Time: 8 hours, Serves: 10

5 cups cooked whole-wheat couscous
4 large carrots, peeled and cut into chunks
2 sweet potatoes, peeled and cubed
2 zucchinis, cut into chunks
2 (10-ounce / 283-g) BPA-free cans no-salt-added

artichoke hearts in water, drained
¼ cup balsamic vinegar
10 garlic cloves, peeled and sliced
2 tbsps. honey
1 tsp. dried marjoram leaves

1. Before getting started, be sure to remove the crisper tray.
2. Mix the carrots, sweet potatoes, garlic, zucchinis, artichoke hearts, vinegar, honey, and marjoram leaves in the bottom of the pot.
3. Close the lid and flip the SmartSwitch to AIRFRY/STOVETOP. Select SLOW COOK, set temperature to "Lo", and set time to 8 hours. Press START/STOP to begin cooking, until the vegetables are soft.
4. Top over the hot cooked couscous and serve.

Parmesan Broccoli (Steam&Crisp)

Prep: 10 minutes, Total Cook Time: 19 minutes, Steam: approx. 4 minutes, Cook: 15 minutes, Serves: 2

½ cup water, for steaming   cooking spray   ⅛ tsp. cayenne pepper

10 ounces frozen broccoli   Salt and black pepper, as required

2 tbsps. Parmesan cheese, grated

3 tbsps. balsamic vinegar   1 tbsp. olive oil

1. Pour ½ cup water into the pot. Push in the legs on the Crisper Tray, then place the tray in the bottom position in the pot.
2. Mix broccoli, vinegar, oil, cayenne, salt, and black pepper in a bowl and toss to coat well. Arrange broccoli on the tray.
3. Close the lid and flip the SmartSwitch to Rapid Cooker. Select STEAM & CRISP, set temperature to 400°F, and set time to 15 minutes. Press START/STOP to begin cooking (the unit will steam for approx. 4 minutes before crisping).
4. With 5 minutes remaining, open the lid and toss the broccoli with tongs. Close the lid to continue cooking.
5. Dish out in a bowl and top with Parmesan cheese to serve.

Almond Asparagus (Bake&Roast)

Prep Time: 15 minutes, Cook Time: 8 minutes, Serves: 3

cooking spray   1 pound asparagus   2 tbsps. balsamic vinegar

⅓ cup almonds, sliced   Salt and black pepper, to taste

2 tbsps. olive oil

1. Push in the legs on the Crisper Tray, then place the tray in the bottom of the pot. Spray the tray with cooking spray.
2. Mix asparagus, oil, vinegar, salt, and black pepper in a bowl and toss to coat well.
3. Close the lid and flip the SmartSwitch to AIRFRY/STOVETOP. Select BAKE & ROAST, set temperature to 390°F, and set time to 13 minutes (unit will need to preheat for 5 minutes, so set an external timer if desired). Press START/STOP to begin cooking.
4. When the unit is preheated and the time reaches 8 minutes, place the asparagus on the tray and sprinkle with the almond slices. Close the lid to begin cooking.
5. After 4 minutes, open the lid and toss the asparagus with silicone-tipped tongs to ensure even cooking. Close the lid to continue cooking.
6. When cooking is complete, serve hot.

Pasta Vegetables Stew (Slow Cook)

Prep Time: 9 minutes, Cook Time: 6½ hours, Serves: 6

1½ cups whole-wheat orzo pasta

6 large tomatoes, seeded and chopped

8 cups vegetable broth

2 cups chopped yellow summer squash

2 cups sliced button mushrooms

2 cups sliced cremini mushrooms

2 red bell peppers, stemmed, seeded, and chopped

2 onions, chopped

5 garlic cloves, minced

2 tsps. dried Italian seasoning

1. Before getting started, be sure to remove the crisper tray.
2. Mix the onions, garlic, mushrooms, bell peppers, summer squash, tomatoes, vegetable broth, and Italian seasoning in the bottom of the pot.
3. Close the lid and flip the SmartSwitch to AIRFRY/STOVETOP. Select SLOW COOK, set temperature to "Lo", and set time to 6 hours. Press START/STOP to begin cooking, until the vegetables are soft.
4. When the time is up, open the lid and place the pasta to the pot, stirring. Close the lid and cook on low for 20 to 30 minutes, until the pasta is tender.
5. Serve warm.

Herbed Succotash with Tomato (Slow Cook)

Prep Time: 14 minutes, Cook Time: 8 hours, Serves: 10

4 cups frozen corn

4 large tomatoes, seeded and chopped

2 cups dry lima beans, rinsed and drained

5 cups vegetable broth

1 red onion, minced

1 bay leaf

1 tsp. dried basil leaves

1 tsp. dried thyme leaves

1. Before getting started, be sure to remove the crisper tray.
2. Mix all the ingredients in the bottom of the pot.
3. Close the lid and flip the SmartSwitch to AIRFRY/STOVETOP. Select SLOW COOK, set temperature to "Lo", and set time to 8 hours. Press START/STOP to begin cooking, until the lima beans are soft.
4. Remove the bay leaf and discard. Serve warm.

Italian Eggplant Parmesan (Slow Cook)

Prep Time: 14 minutes, Cook Time: 8 hours, Serves: 8 to 10

2 tbsps. olive oil

5 large eggplants, peeled and sliced ½-inch thick

2 (8-ounce / 227-g) BPA-free cans low-sodium tomato sauce

2 onions, chopped   ½ cup chopped toasted almonds

½ cup grated Parmesan cheese   6 garlic cloves, minced

1 tsp. dried Italian seasoning

1. Before getting started, be sure to remove the crisper tray.
2. Layer the eggplant slices with the onions and garlic in the bottom of the pot.
3. Mix the tomato sauce, olive oil, and Italian seasoning in a medium bowl. Add the tomato sauce mixture into the pot.
4. Close the lid and flip the SmartSwitch to AIRFRY/STOVETOP. Select SLOW COOK, set temperature to "Lo", and set time to 8 hours. Press START/STOP to begin cooking, until the eggplant is soft.
5. Mix the Parmesan cheese and almonds in a small bowl. Scatter over the eggplant mixture and serve warm.

Sous Vide Glazed Carrots (Sous Vide)

Prep Time: 4 minutes, Cook Time: 45 minutes, Serves: 3

4-5 carrots of different colors, peeled, sliced   Salt/Pepper

1 tsp. of dried thyme   1 tbsp. of salted butter

1. Before getting started, remove the crisper tray and add 12 cups of room-temperature water to the pot (reference the marking on the inside of the pot).
2. Close the lid and flip the SmartSwitch to AIRFRY/STOVETOP. Select SOUS VIDE, set temperature to 180°F, and set time to 45 minutes.
3. Press START/STOP to begin preheating.(Time for preheating depends on the temperature of the water added.)
4. Place the carrots in a Sous Vide bag.
5. When preheating is complete and "ADD FOOD" will show on the display.
6. Open the lid and place bag in the water using the water displacement method. When just the bag's seal is above the water line, finish closing the bag, making sure no water gets inside. Keep the bag's seal just above the water line.
7. Close the lid.
8. When cooking is complete, remove the carrots from the bag and glaze in a pan with the butter and thyme until they get a sleek golden sheen.
9. Serve warm.

CHAPTER 4:
FISH AND SEAFOOD RECIPES

Spiced Catfish with Spaghetti (Speedi Meals)

Prep: 15 minutes, Total Cook Time: 25 minutes, Steam: approx. 10 minutes, Cook: 15 minutes, Serves: 4

LEVEL 1 (BOTTOM OF POT)
10 ounces spaghetti pasta, broken in half

3 cups water   1 cup tomato sauce

LEVEL 2 (TRAY)
4 (6-ounces) catfish fillets   1 tbsp. olive oil

2 tbsps. corn meal   2 tbsps. corn flour

2 tbsps. garlic   2 tbsps. Salt

TOPPINGS:

Tzatziki   Guacamole

1. Place all Level 1 ingredients in the pot and stir to combine.
2. Pull out the legs on the Crisper Tray, then place the tray in the elevated position in the pot.
3. Mix the catfish fillets with corn meal, corn flour, garlic and salt in a bowl.
4. Drizzle with olive oil and arrange catfish fillets on top of the tray.
5. Close the lid and flip the SmartSwitch to RAPID COOKER.
6. Select SPEEDI MEALS, set temperature to 350°F, and set time to 15 minutes. Press START/ STOP to begin cooking (the unit will steam for approx. 10 minutes before crisping).
7. When cooking is complete, remove the catfish fillets from the tray. Then use silicone-tipped tongs to grab the center handle and remove the tray from the unit. Transfer the spaghetti pasta to a bowl, then top with the catfish fillets and desired toppings.

Tasty Mahi Mahi Meal (Speedi Meals)

Prep: 15 minutes, Total Cook Time: 25 minutes, Steam: approx. 10 minutes, Cook: 15 minutes, Serves: 3

LEVEL 1 (BOTTOM OF POT)
1 cup jasmine rice, rinsed   1½ cups water

1 cup frozen mixed vegetables

LEVEL 2 (TRAY)

1½ pounds Mahi Mahi fillets slices   1 lemon, cut into

1 tbsp. fresh dill, chopped   ½ tsp. red chili powder

Salt and ground black pepper, as required

1. Place all Level 1 ingredients in the pot and stir to combine.
2. Pull out the legs on the Crisper Tray, then place the tray in the elevated position in the pot.
3. Season the Mahi Mahi fillets evenly with chili powder, salt, and black pepper. Arrange the Mahi Mahi fillets on top of the tray and top with the lemon slices.
4. Close the lid and flip the SmartSwitch to RAPID COOKER.
5. Select SPEEDI MEALS, set temperature to 350°F, and set time to 15 minutes. Press START/STOP to begin cooking (the unit will steam for approx. 10 minutes before crisping).
6. When cooking is complete, remove the Mahi Mahi fillets and lemon slices from the tray. Then use silicone-tipped tongs to grab the center handle and remove the tray from the unit. Transfer the rice and vegetables to a bowl, then top with the Mahi Mahi fillets and lemon slices. Garnish with fresh dill and serve warm.

Spicy Cod (Steam&Crisp)

Prep: 10 minutes, Total Cook Time: 12 minutes, Steam: approx. 4 minutes, Cook: 8 minutes, Serves: 2

¼ cup water, for steaming
2 (6-ounces) (1½-inch thick) cod fillets
1 tsp. smoked paprika   1 tsp. cayenne pepper
1 tsp. onion powder   1 tsp. garlic powder

Salt and ground black pepper, as required
2 tsps. olive oil

1. Pour ¼ cup water into the pot. Pull out the legs on the Crisper Tray, then place the tray in the elevated position in the pot.
2. Drizzle the cod fillets with olive oil and rub with the all the spices.
3. Arrange the cod fillets on the tray.
4. Close the lid and flip the SmartSwitch to Rapid Cooker. Select STEAM & CRISP, set temperature to 450°F, and set time to 8 minutes. Press START/STOP to begin cooking (the unit will steam for approx. 4 minutes before crisping).
5. With 4 minutes remaining, open the lid and toss the cod fillets with tongs. Close the lid to continue cooking.
6. When cooking is complete, use tongs to remove the cod fillets from the tray and serve hot.

Amazing Salmon Fillets (Steam&Crisp)

Prep: 5 minutes, Total Cook Time: 12 minutes, Steam: approx. 4 minutes, Cook: 8 minutes, Serves: 2

¼ cup water, for steaming
2 (7-ounce) (¾-inch thick) salmon fillets

1 tbsp. Italian seasoning
1 tbsp. fresh lemon juice

1. Pour ¼ cup water into the pot. Pull out the legs on the Crisper Tray, then place the tray in the elevated position in the pot.
2. Rub the salmon evenly with Italian seasoning and transfer on the tray, skin-side up.
3. Close the lid and flip the SmartSwitch to Rapid Cooker. Select STEAM & CRISP, set temperature to 450°F, and set time to 8 minutes. Press START/STOP to begin cooking (the unit will steam for approx. 4 minutes before crisping).
4. With 4 minutes remaining, open the lid and flip the salmon with tongs. Close the lid to continue cooking.
5. When cooking is complete, use tongs to remove the salmon from the tray. Squeeze lemon juice on it to serve.

Sweet and Sour Glazed Cod (Steam&Crisp)

Prep: 20 minutes, Total Cook Time: 14 minutes, Steam: approx. 4 minutes, Cook: 10 minutes, Serves: 2

½ cup water, for steaming
4 (3½-ounces) cod fillets

1 tsp. water   ⅓ cup soy sauce
⅓ cup honey   3 tsps. rice wine vinegar

1. Mix the soy sauce, honey, vinegar and 1 tsp. water in a small bowl. Reserve about half of the mixture in another bowl. Stir the cod fillets in the remaining mixture until well coated. Cover and refrigerate to marinate for about 3 hours.
2. Pour ½ cup water into the pot. Pull out the legs on the Crisper Tray, then place the tray in the elevated position in the pot.
3. Arrange the cod fillets on the tray.
4. Close the lid and flip the SmartSwitch to Rapid Cooker. Select STEAM & CRISP, set temperature to 450°F, and set time to 10 minutes. Press START/STOP to begin cooking (the unit will steam for approx. 4 minutes before crisping).
5. With 5 minutes remaining, open the lid and flip the cod with tongs. Close the lid to continue cooking.
6. When cooking is complete, use tongs to remove the cod from the tray.
7. Coat with the reserved marinade and serve hot.

Spicy Orange Shrimp (Air Fry)

Prep Time: 20 minutes, Cook Time: 10 minutes, Serves: 4

⅓ cup orange juice   3 tsps. minced garlic
1 tsp. Old Bay seasoning
¼ to ½ tsp. cayenne pepper

1 pound (454 g) medium shrimp, peeled and deveined, with tails off
Cooking spray

1. In a medium bowl, combine the orange juice, garlic, Old Bay seasoning, and cayenne pepper.
2. Dry the shrimp with paper towels to remove excess water.
3. Add the shrimp to the marinade and stir to evenly coat. Cover with plastic wrap and place in the refrigerator for 30 minutes so the shrimp can soak up the marinade.
4. Push in the legs on the Crisper Tray, then place the tray in the bottom of the pot. Spray the tray with cooking spray.
5. Close the lid and flip the SmartSwitch to AIRFRY/STOVETOP. Select AIRFRY, set temperature to 390°F, and set time to 15 minutes (unit will need to preheat for 5 minutes, so set an external timer if desired). Press START/STOP to begin cooking.
6. When the unit is preheated and the time reaches 10 minutes, place the shrimp on the tray. Close the lid to begin cooking.
7. After 5 minutes, open the lid. Flip the shrimp and lightly spray with cooking spray. Close the lid to continue cooking.
8. Serve immediately.

Cheesy Shrimp (Air Fry)

Prep Time: 20 minutes, Cook Time: 14 minutes, Serves: 4

cooking spray   ⅔ cup Parmesan cheese, grated
2 pounds shrimp, peeled and deveined
4 garlic cloves, minced   2 tbsps. olive oil
1 tsp. dried basil   ½ tsp. dried oregano

1 tsp. onion powder
½ tsp. red pepper flakes, crushed
Ground black pepper, as required
2 tbsps. fresh lemon juice

1. Push in the legs on the Crisper Tray, then place the tray in the bottom of the pot. Spray the tray with cooking spray.
2. Mix Parmesan cheese, garlic, olive oil, herbs, and spices in a large bowl and stir in the shrimp.
3. Close the lid and flip the SmartSwitch to AIRFRY/STOVETOP. Select AIRFRY, set temperature to 390°F, and set time to 12 minutes (unit will need to preheat for 5 minutes, so set an external timer if desired). Press START/STOP to begin cooking.
4. When the unit is preheated and the time reaches 7 minutes, place half of the shrimp on the tray. Close the lid to begin cooking.
5. Repeat with the remaining shrimp.
6. Dish out the shrimp onto serving plates and drizzle with lemon juice to serve hot.

Herbed Haddock (Bake&Roast)

Prep Time: 10 minutes, Cook Time: 8 minutes, Serves: 2

cooking spray   2 (6-ounce) haddock fillets
2 tbsps. pine nuts
3 tbsps. fresh basil, chopped

1 tbsp. Parmesan cheese, grated
½ cup extra-virgin olive oil
Salt and black pepper, to taste

1. Push in the legs on the Crisper Tray, then place the tray in the bottom of the pot. Spray the tray with cooking spray.
2. Coat the haddock fillets evenly with olive oil and season with salt and black pepper.
3. Close the lid and flip the SmartSwitch to AIRFRY/STOVETOP. Select BAKE & ROAST, set temperature to 390°F, and set time to 13 minutes (unit will need to preheat for 5 minutes, so set an external timer if desired). Press START/STOP to begin cooking.
4. When the unit is preheated and the time reaches 8 minutes, place the haddock fillets on the tray. Close the lid to begin cooking.
5. After 4 minutes, open the lid and flip the haddock fillets with silicone-tipped tongs to ensure even cooking. Close the lid to continue cooking.
6. Meanwhile, put remaining ingredients in a food processor and pulse until smooth.
7. Top this cheese sauce over the haddock fillets and serve hot.

Cajun Spiced Salmon (Bake&Roast)

Prep Time: 10 minutes, Cook Time: 10 minutes, Serves: 2

cooking spray   2 (7-ounces) (¾-inch thick) salmon fillets
1 tbsp. Cajun seasoning   ½ tsp. coconut sugar   1 tbsp. fresh lemon juice

1. Push in the legs on the Crisper Tray, then place the tray in the bottom of the pot. Spray the tray with cooking spray.
2. Season the salmon evenly with Cajun seasoning and coconut sugar.
3. Close the lid and flip the SmartSwitch to AIRFRY/STOVETOP. Select BAKE & ROAST, set temperature to 390°F, and set time to 15 minutes (unit will need to preheat for 5 minutes, so set an external timer if desired). Press START/STOP to begin cooking.
4. When the unit is preheated and the time reaches 10 minutes, place the salmon fillets on the tray, skin-side up. Close the lid to begin cooking.
5. After 5 minutes, open the lid and flip the salmon fillets with silicone-tipped tongs to ensure even cooking. Close the lid to continue cooking.
6. Drizzle with the lemon juice and serve hot.

White Fish and Spinach Risotto (Slow Cook)

Prep Time: 7 minutes, Cook Time: 4 hours 40 minutes, Serves: 4

2 cups short-grain brown rice
6 (5-ounce / 142-g) tilapia fillets
8 ounces (227 g) cremini mushrooms, sliced
6 cups vegetable broth or fish stock
2 cups baby spinach leaves
2 onions, chopped

½ cup grated Parmesan cheese
5 garlic cloves, minced
2 tbsps. unsalted butter
1 tsp. dried thyme leaves

1. Before getting started, be sure to remove the crisper tray.
2. Mix the mushrooms, onions, garlic, rice, thyme, and vegetable broth in the bottom of the pot.
3. Close the lid and flip the SmartSwitch to AIRFRY/STOVETOP. Select SLOW COOK, set temperature to "Lo", and set time to 4 hours. Press START/STOP to begin cooking, until the rice is soft.
4. When the time is up, open the lid and place the fish on top of the rice. Close the lid and cook on low for another 30 minutes, or until the fish flakes when tested with a fork.
5. Gently place the fish into the risotto. Then put the baby spinach leaves.
6. Stir in the butter and cheese. Cover and allow to cook on low for 10 minutes, then Serve warm.

Shrimp and Grits with Tomato (Slow Cook)

Prep Time: 16 minutes, Cook Time: 6½ hours, Serves: 9

2 pounds (907 g) raw shrimp, peeled and deveined
4 large tomatoes, seeded and chopped
2½ cups stone-ground grits
8 cups chicken stock or vegetable broth
2 onions, chopped
2 green bell peppers, stemmed, seeded, and

chopped
1½ cups shredded Cheddar cheese
5 garlic cloves, minced
1 bay leaf
1 tsp. Old Bay Seasoning

1. Before getting started, be sure to remove the crisper tray.
2. Mix the grits, onions, garlic, tomatoes, bell peppers, chicken stock, bay leaf, and seasoning in the bottom of the pot.
3. Close the lid and flip the SmartSwitch to AIRFRY/STOVETOP. Select SLOW COOK, set temperature to "Lo", and set time to 6 hours. Press START/STOP to begin cooking, until the grits are soft and most of the liquid is absorbed.
4. When the time is up, open the lid and place the shrimp, stirring. Close the lid and cook on low for 30 to 40 minutes, until the shrimp are curled and pink.
5. Stir in the cheese and serve warm.

Garlic Squid (Sous Vide)

Prep Time: 10 minutes, Cook Time: 2 hours, Serves: 4

4 small clean squids   2 garlic cloves, chopped   2 tbsps. olive oil   Salt and pepper to taste

1. Before getting started, remove the crisper tray and add 12 cups of room-temperature water to the pot (reference the marking on the inside of the pot).
2. Close the lid and flip the SmartSwitch to AIRFRY/STOVETOP. Select SOUS VIDE, set temperature to 130°F, and set time to 2 hours.
3. Press START/STOP to begin preheating.(Time for preheating depends on the temperature of the water added.)
4. Season the squid with salt and put into a Sous Vide bag. Add olive oil and chopped garlic.
5. When preheating is complete and "ADD FOOD" will show on the display.
6. Open the lid and place bag in the water using the water displacement method. When just the bag's seal is above the water line, finish closing the bag, making sure no water gets inside. Keep the bag's seal just above the water line.
7. Close the lid.
8. When cooking is complete, remove the bag with squid from cooker.
9. Serve sprinkled with lemon juice.

CHAPTER 5:

PORK RECIPES

Five Spice Pork and Quinoa with Asparagus (Speedi Meals)

Prep: 15 minutes, Total Cook Time: 30 minutes, Steam: approx. 10 minutes, Cook: 20 minutes, Serves: 4

LEVEL 1 (BOTTOM OF POT)
1 cup quinoa, rinsed
1 small bunch asparagus, trimmed
1½ cups water   1 tbsp. olive oil
Salt and ground black pepper, as required

LEVEL 2 (TRAY)
1-pound pork belly   2 tbsps. swerve

2 tbsps. dark soy sauce
1 tbsp. Shaoxing (cooking wine)
2 tsps. garlic, minced   2 tsps. ginger, minced
1 tbsp. hoisin sauce   1 tsp. Chinese Five Spice

TOPPINGS:
Hummus   Sesame seeds

1. Place all Level 1 ingredients in the pot and stir to combine.
2. Pull out the legs on the Crisper Tray, then place the tray in the elevated position in the pot.
3. Mix all the ingredients in a bowl and place in the Ziplock bag.
4. Seal the bag, shake it well and refrigerate to marinate for about 1 hour.
5. Remove the pork from the bag and arrange on top of the tray.
6. Close the lid and flip the SmartSwitch to RAPID COOKER.
7. Select SPEEDI MEALS, set temperature to 375°F, and set time to 20 minutes. Press START/STOP to begin cooking (the unit will steam for approx. 10 minutes before crisping).
8. When cooking is complete, remove the pork from the tray. Then use silicone-tipped tongs to grab the center handle and remove the tray from the unit. Transfer the quinoa and asparagus to a bowl, then top with the pork and desired toppings.

Breaded Pork Chops and Cherry Tomato Pasta (Speedi Meals)

Prep: 15 minutes, Total Cook Time: 25 minutes, Steam: approx. 10 minutes, Cook: 15 minutes, Serves: 2

LEVEL 1 (BOTTOM OF POT)
8 ounces Plain pasta   2 cups water
½ cup tomato sauce   ½ cup cherry tomatoes
½ cup fresh zucchini, chopped

LEVEL 2 (TRAY)
2 (6-ounces) pork chops   ¼ cup plain flour

1 egg   4 ounces breadcrumbs
Salt and black pepper, to taste
1 tbsp. vegetable oil

TOPPINGS:
Fresh basil   Greek yogurt

1. Place all Level 1 ingredients in the pot and stir to combine.
2. Pull out the legs on the Crisper Tray, then place the tray in the elevated position in the pot.
3. Season the chops with salt and black pepper. Place the flour in a shallow bowl and whisk an egg in a second bowl. Mix the breadcrumbs and vegetable oil in a third bowl.
4. Coat the pork chops with flour, dip into egg and dredge into the breadcrumb mixture. Arrange the chops on top of the tray.
5. Close the lid and flip the SmartSwitch to RAPID COOKER.
6. Select SPEEDI MEALS, set temperature to 375°F, and set time to 15 minutes. Press START/STOP to begin cooking (the unit will steam for approx. 10 minutes before crisping).
7. When cooking is complete, remove the pork chops from the tray. Then use silicone-tipped tongs to grab the center handle and remove the tray from the unit. Transfer the pasta and vegetables to a bowl, then top with the pork chops and desired toppings.

Coffee-Chili Pork Porterhouse (Sous Vide)

Prep Time: 20 minutes, Cook Time: 2 hours 30 minutes, Serves: 4

2 pieces bone-in pork porterhouse

1 tbsp. ancho chilis powder

1 tbsp. ground coffee

1 tbsp. light brown sugar

1 tbsp. extra-virgin olive oil

1 tbsp. garlic salt

1. Before getting started, remove the crisper tray and add 12 cups of room-temperature water to the pot (reference the marking on the inside of the pot).
2. Close the lid and flip the SmartSwitch to AIRFRY/STOVETOP. Select SOUS VIDE, set temperature to 145°F, and set time to 2½ hours.
3. Press START/STOP to begin preheating.(Time for preheating depends on the temperature of the water added.)
4. Add the pork to a Sous Vide bag.
5. When preheating is complete and "ADD FOOD" will show on the display.
6. Open the lid and place bag in the water using the water displacement method. When just the bag's seal is above the water line, finish closing the bag, making sure no water gets inside. Keep the bag's seal just above the water line.
7. Close the lid.
8. Make your seasoning mixture by adding the chili powder, coffee, brown sugar, and garlic salt to a small bowl.
9. When cooking is complete, remove the bag with pork from cooker.
10. Then take the pork out from the bag, pat it dry using kitchen towel.
11. Rub the chop with seasoning.
12. Take a cast iron skillet and put it over high heat and add the olive oil and sear the pork for 1-2 minutes per side.
13. Once done, transfer the pork to a cutting board and allow it to rest for 5 minutes, slice and serve!

Cheese Crusted Chops (Air Fry)

Prep Time: 10 minutes, Cook Time: 18 minutes, Serves: 4 to 6

¼ tsp. pepper   ½ tsp. salt

4 to 6 thick boneless pork chops

1 cup pork rind crumbs

¼ tsp. chili powder   ½ tsp. onion powder

1 tsp. smoked paprika   2 beaten eggs

3 tbsps. grated Parmesan cheese

Cooking spray

1. Push in the legs on the Crisper Tray, then place the tray in the bottom of the pot. Spray the tray with cooking spray.
2. Rub the pepper and salt on both sides of pork chops.
3. In a food processor, pulse pork rinds into crumbs. Mix crumbs with chili powder, onion powder, and paprika in a bowl. Beat eggs in another bowl. Dip pork chops into eggs then into pork rind crumb mixture.
4. Close the lid and flip the SmartSwitch to AIRFRY/STOVETOP. Select AIRFRY, set temperature to 375°F, and set time to 23 minutes (unit will need to preheat for 5 minutes, so set an external timer if desired). Press START/STOP to begin cooking.
5. When the unit is preheated and the time reaches 18 minutes, place the pork chops on the tray. Close the lid to begin cooking.
6. After 10 minutes, open the lid and flip the pork chops with silicone-tipped tongs to ensure even cooking. Close the lid to continue cooking.
7. When cooking is complete, serve garnished with the Parmesan cheese.

Thai Pork and Mushroom with Peanut Sauce (Slow Cook)

Prep Time: 22 minutes, Cook Time: 8 hours, Serves: 8

1 (3-pound / 1.4-kg) boneless pork loin roast
2 cups chopped portabello mushrooms
2 onions, chopped
1 cup chopped unsalted peanuts
1 cup peanut butter   1 cup chicken stock

4 garlic cloves, minced
1 small dried red chili pepper, sliced
2 tbsps. apple cider vinegar
¼ tsp. cayenne pepper

1. Before getting started, be sure to remove the crisper tray.
2. Mix the onions, mushrooms, garlic, chili pepper, and cayenne pepper in the bottom of the pot.
3. In a medium bowl, mix the chicken stock, peanut butter, and vinegar and mix until well blended.
4. Put the pork roast on top of the vegetables in the pot. Pour the peanut butter sauce over all.
5. Close the lid and flip the SmartSwitch to AIRFRY/STOVETOP. Select SLOW COOK, set temperature to "Lo", and set time to 8 hours. Press START/STOP to begin cooking, until the pork is very tender.
6. Scatter with peanuts and serve warm.

Thai Pork with Basil (Sear/Sauté)

Prep Time: 7 minutes, Cook Time: 5 minutes, Serves: 4

1 pound (454 g) ground pork
1 medium red bell pepper, cut into ½-inch pieces
1 handful fresh Thai basil leaves
2 garlic cloves, crushed and chopped
2 tbsps. cooking oil

1 tbsp. ginger, crushed and chopped
1 tbsp. fish sauce   2 tbsps. brown sugar
1 tbsp. soy sauce

1. Before getting started, be sure to remove the Crisper Tray from the pot.
2. Flip the SmartSwitch to AIRFRY/STOVETOP. Select SEAR/SAUTÉ, choose "Hi5". Press START/STOP to begin cooking.
3. Heat the cooking oil in the pot until it shimmers.
4. Add the garlic, ginger and pork and sear for about 2 minutes.
5. Pour the bell pepper, brown sugar, fish sauce and soy sauce and sauté for about 1 minute.
6. Sprinkle the basil and sauté until just wilted.
7. Serve warm.

Sweet and Sour Pork and Pineapple (Sear/Sauté)

Prep Time: 15 minutes, Cook Time: 6 minutes, Serves: 5

1 pound (454 g) pork tenderloin, cut into 1-inch pieces

1 (8-ounce / 227-g) can pineapple chunks, drained, juice reserved

1 red bell pepper, cut into 1-inch pieces

1 medium red onion, cut into 1-inch pieces

4 scallions, cut into 1-inch pieces

2 garlic cloves, crushed and chopped

¼ cup cooking oil

¼ cup plus 2 tbsps. cornstarch, divided

¼ cup rice vinegar   2 tbsps. brown sugar

1 tbsp. ginger, crushed and chopped

1. Whisk together the reserved pineapple juice, rice vinegar, 2 tbsps. of the cornstarch, and brown sugar in a small bowl. Set aside.
2. Put the pork to a resealable plastic bag or covered bowl. Toss with the remaining ¼ cup of cornstarch to coat fully.
3. Before getting started, be sure to remove the Crisper Tray from the pot.
4. Flip the SmartSwitch to AIRFRY/STOVETOP. Select SEAR/SAUTÉ, choose "Hi5". Press START/STOP to begin cooking.
5. Heat the cooking oil in the pot until it shimmers.
6. Add the garlic and ginger and sear for about 1 minute.
7. Place the pork and shallow-fry until lightly browned. Remove the pork and keep aside.
8. Remove and discard all but 2 tbsps. of oil from the pot.
9. Arrange the onion to the pot and sauté for 1 minute.
10. Then put the bell pepper and pineapple chunks and sauté for 1 minute.
11. Pour in the pineapple juice mixture and stir until a glaze is formed. Stir in the cooked pork.
12. Sprinkle with the scallions and serve warm.

Pork Hoagies (Sous Vide)

Prep Time: 15 minutes, Cook Time: 12 hours, Serves: 4

1 lb. boneless pork shoulder chops

1 tbsp. dry rub + additional tsp. for later use

¼ cup BBQ sauce   4 hoagie rolls

1 cup prepped fried pickles for topping

1. Before getting started, remove the crisper tray and add 12 cups of room-temperature water to the pot (reference the marking on the inside of the pot).
2. Close the lid and flip the SmartSwitch to AIRFRY/STOVETOP. Select SOUS VIDE, set temperature to 165°F, and set time to 12 hours.
3. Press START/STOP to begin preheating.(Time for preheating depends on the temperature of the water added.)
4. Slice up the pork into bite-sized portions and season with 1 tbsp. of dry rub.
5. Transfer the chops to a Sous Vide bag.
6. When preheating is complete and "ADD FOOD" will show on the display.
7. Open the lid and place bag in the water using the water displacement method. When just the bag's seal is above the water line, finish closing the bag, making sure no water gets inside. Keep the bag's seal just above the water line.
8. Close the lid.
9. Once cooked, remove the pork from the bag and shred it.
10. Season using the dry rub.
11. Serve by topping the hoagie rolls with soft fried pickles and a drizzle of BBQ sauce.

Sesame Pork and Carrot (Sear/Sauté)

Prep Time: 8 minutes, Cook Time: 5 minutes, Serves: 4

1 pound (454 g) pork tenderloin, cut into 1-inch pieces
1 medium carrot, roll-cut into ½-inch pieces
1 medium onion, cut into 1-inch pieces
1 medium red bell pepper, cut into 1-inch pieces
4 scallions, cut into 1-inch pieces

2 garlic cloves, crushed and chopped
2 tbsps. cooking oil   2 tbsps. sesame seeds
2 tbsps. soy sauce   2 tbsps. honey
1 tbsp. cornstarch   1 tsp. hot sesame oil
1 tbsp. ginger, crushed and chopped

1. Before getting started, be sure to remove the Crisper Tray from the pot.
2. Flip the SmartSwitch to AIRFRY/STOVETOP. Select SEAR/SAUTÉ, choose "Hi5". Press START/STOP to begin cooking.
3. Heat the cooking oil in the pot until it shimmers.
4. Add the garlic, ginger and carrot and sear for about 1 minute.
5. Place the pork and sauté for about 1 minute.
6. Then put the onion and bell pepper and sauté for about 1 minute.
7. Pour the sesame oil, honey, soy sauce and cornstarch and stir until a light glaze is formed.
8. Sprinkle with the sesame seeds and scallions. Serve warm.

Cheesy Sausage Balls and Bulgur Wheat (Speedi Meals)

Prep: 10 minutes, Total Cook Time: 25 minutes, Steam: approx. 10 minutes, Cook: 15 minutes, Serves: 4

LEVEL 1 (BOTTOM OF POT)
1 cup easy-cooked Bulgur wheat, rinsed
2 cups water   1 cup fresh sweet potato, chopped
LEVEL 2 (TRAY)
12 ounces (340 g) Jimmy Dean's Sausage

6 ounces (170 g) shredded Cheddar cheese
12 Cheddar cubes
TOPPINGS:
Mustard   Pesto

1. Place all Level 1 ingredients in the pot and stir to combine.
2. Pull out the legs on the Crisper Tray, then place the tray in the elevated position in the pot.
3. Mix the shredded cheese and sausage. Divide the mixture into 12 equal parts to be stuffed.
4. Add a cube of cheese to the center of the sausage and roll into balls. Place the balls on top of the tray.
5. Close the lid and flip the SmartSwitch to RAPID COOKER.
6. Select SPEEDI MEALS, set temperature to 375°F, and set time to 15 minutes. Press START/STOP to begin cooking (the unit will steam for approx. 10 minutes before crisping).
7. When cooking is complete, remove the sausage balls from the tray. Then use silicone-tipped tongs to grab the center handle and remove the tray from the unit. Transfer the Bulgur wheat and sweet potato to a bowl, then top with the sausage balls and desired toppings.

Pork and Brussels Sprouts with Oyster Sauce (Sear/Sauté)

Prep Time: 12 minutes, Cook Time: 5 minutes, Serves: 4

1 pound (454 g) ground pork   1 dozen Brussels sprouts, trimmed and halved
1 medium onion, diced   ¼ cup oyster sauce   ¼ cup honey
2 tbsps. cooking oil   2 garlic cloves, crushed and chopped
1 tbsp. ginger, crushed and chopped

1. Before getting started, be sure to remove the Crisper Tray from the pot.
2. Flip the SmartSwitch to AIRFRY/STOVETOP. Select SEAR/SAUTÉ, choose "Hi5". Press START/STOP to begin cooking.
3. Heat the cooking oil in the pot until it shimmers.
4. Add the garlic, ginger and brussels sprouts and sear for about 1 minute.
5. Place the pork, onion and honey and sauté for about 2 minutes.
6. Add the oyster sauce and toss for about 30 seconds.
7. Serve warm.

CHAPTER 6:
BEEF RECIPES

Avocado Buttered Flank Steak with Pea Rice (Speedi Meals)

Prep: 10 minutes, Total Cook Time: 22 minutes, Steam: approx. 12 minutes, Cook: 10 minutes, Serves: 2

LEVEL 1 (BOTTOM OF POT)
1 cup jasmine rice, rinsed
2 red bell peppers, sliced thin
½ cup peas   2 cups water
1 tbsp. olive oil

LEVEL 2 (TRAY)
1 flank steak
Salt and ground black pepper, to taste
2 avocados   2 tbsps. butter, melted
½ cup chimichurri sauce

TOPPINGS:
Tzatziki   Fresh chopped parsley

1. Place all Level 1 ingredients in the pot and stir to combine.
2. Pull out the legs on the Crisper Tray, then place the tray in the elevated position in the pot.
3. Halve the avocados and take out the pits. Spoon the flesh into a bowl and mash with a fork. Mix in the melted butter and chimichurri sauce, making sure everything is well combined. Put the steak on top of the tray.
4. Close the lid and flip the SmartSwitch to RAPID COOKER.
5. Select SPEEDI MEALS, set temperature to 375°F, and set time to 12 minutes. Press START/STOP to begin cooking (the unit will steam for approx. 10 minutes before crisping).
6. When cooking is complete, remove the steak from the tray. Then use silicone-tipped tongs to grab the center handle and remove the tray from the unit. Transfer the rice and vegetables to a bowl, then top with the steak and desired toppings.

Easy Rib Steak and Broccoli Risotto (Speedi Meals)

Prep: 15 minutes, Total Cook Time: 30 minutes, Steam: approx. 10 minutes, Cook: 20 minutes, Serves: 4

LEVEL 1 (BOTTOM OF POT)
1 cup Arborio rice
1 cup frozen broccoli florets
3½ cups water or stock
2 tbsps. salted butter, cubed
Salt and black pepper, to taste

LEVEL 2 (TRAY)
2 lbs. rib steak   2 cup steak rub
1 tbsp. olive oil

TOPPINGS:
Hummus   Salsa

1. Place all Level 1 ingredients in the pot and stir to combine.
2. Pull out the legs on the Crisper Tray, then place the tray in the elevated position in the pot.
3. Rub the steak generously with steak rub, salt and black pepper, and coat with olive oil. Transfer the steak on top of the tray.
4. Close the lid and flip the SmartSwitch to RAPID COOKER.
5. Select SPEEDI MEALS, set temperature to 375°F, and set time to 20 minutes. Press START/STOP to begin cooking (the unit will steam for approx. 10 minutes before crisping).
6. When cooking is complete, remove the steak from the tray. Then use silicone-tipped tongs to grab the center handle and remove the tray from the unit. Transfer the rice and broccoli to a bowl, then top with the steak and desired toppings.

Miso Marinated Steak and Spinach Pasta (Speedi Meals)

Prep: 15 minutes, Total Cook Time: 25 minutes, Steam: approx. 10 minutes, Cook: 15 minutes, Serves: 2

LEVEL 1 (BOTTOM OF POT)
8 ounces legume based pasta
2 cups spinach   3 cups water

LEVEL 2 (TRAY)
cooking spray   ¾ pound (340 g) flank steak

1½ tbsps. sake   1 tbsp. brown miso paste
1 tsp. honey   2 cloves garlic, pressed
1 tbsp. olive oil

TOPPINGS:
Sesame seeds   Sour cream

1. Place all Level 1 ingredients in the pot and stir to combine.
2. Pull out the legs on the Crisper Tray, then place the tray in the elevated position in the pot.
3. Put all Level 2 ingredients in a Ziploc bag. Shake to cover the steak well with the seasonings and refrigerate for at least 1 hour.
4. Coat all sides of the steak with cooking spray. Put the steak on top of the tray.
5. Close the lid and flip the SmartSwitch to RAPID COOKER.
6. Select SPEEDI MEALS, set temperature to 375°F, and set time to 15 minutes. Press START/STOP to begin cooking (the unit will steam for approx. 10 minutes before crisping).
7. When cooking is complete, remove the steak from the tray. Then use silicone-tipped tongs to grab the center handle and remove the tray from the unit. Transfer the pasta and spinach to a bowl, then top with the steak and desired toppings.

Crumbed Golden Filet Mignon (Air Fry)

Prep Time: 15 minutes, Cook Time: 12 minutes, Serves: 4

cooking spray   ½ pound (227 g) filet mignon
Sea salt and ground black pepper, to taste
½ tsp. cayenne pepper   1 tsp. dried basil

1 tsp. dried rosemary   1 tsp. dried thyme
1 tbsp. sesame oil   1 small egg, whisked
½ cup bread crumbs

1. Mix the filet mignon with the salt, black pepper, cayenne pepper, basil, rosemary, and thyme. Coat with sesame oil.
2. Put the egg in a shallow plate. Pour the bread crumbs in another plate. Dip the filet mignon into the egg. Roll it into the crumbs.
3. Push in the legs on the Crisper Tray, then place the tray in the bottom of the pot. Spray the tray with cooking spray.
4. Close the lid and flip the SmartSwitch to AIRFRY/STOVETOP. Select AIRFRY, set temperature to 375°F, and set time to 17 minutes (unit will need to preheat for 5 minutes, so set an external timer if desired). Press START/STOP to begin cooking.
5. When the unit is preheated and the time reaches 12 minutes, place the steak on the tray. Close the lid to begin cooking.
6. After 6 minutes, open the lid and flip the steak with silicone-tipped tongs to ensure even cooking. Close the lid to continue cooking.
7. Serve immediately.

Beef and Veggie Kebabs (Bake&Roast)

Prep Time: 20 minutes, Cook Time: 12 minutes, Serves: 4

cooking spray
1 pound sirloin steak, cut into-inch chunks
8 ounces baby Bella mushrooms, stems removed
1 large bell pepper, seeded and cut into 1-inch pieces

1 red onion, cut into 1-inch pieces
¼ cup soy sauce   ¼ cup olive oil
1 tbsp. garlic, minced   1 tsp. coconut sugar
½ tsp. ground cumin
Salt and black pepper, to taste

1. Mix soy sauce, oil, garlic, coconut sugar, cumin, salt, and black pepper in a large bowl.
2. Coat the steak cubes generously with marinade and refrigerate to marinate for about 30 minutes.
3. Thread the steak cubes, mushrooms, bell pepper, and onion onto metal skewers.
4. Push in the legs on the Crisper Tray, then place the tray in the bottom of the pot. Spray the tray with cooking spray.
5. Close the lid and flip the SmartSwitch to AIRFRY/STOVETOP. Select BAKE & ROAST, set temperature to 390°F, and set time to 17 minutes (unit will need to preheat for 5 minutes, so set an external timer if desired). Press START/STOP to begin cooking.
6. When the unit is preheated and the time reaches 12 minutes, place the skewers on the tray. Close the lid to begin cooking.
7. After 6 minutes, open the lid and flip the skewers with silicone-tipped tongs to ensure even cooking. Close the lid to continue cooking.
8. Dish out in a platter and serve hot.

Holiday Spicy Beef Roast (Bake&Roast)

Prep Time: 10 minutes, Cook Time: 45 minutes, Serves: 8

cooking spray
2 pounds (907 g) roast beef, at room temperature
2 tbsps. extra-virgin olive oil
1 tsp. sea salt flakes

1 tsp. black pepper, preferably freshly ground
1 tsp. smoked paprika A few dashes of liquid smoke
2 jalapeño peppers, thinly sliced

1. Push in the legs on the Crisper Tray, then place the tray in the bottom of the pot. Spray the tray with cooking spray.
2. Pat the roast dry using kitchen towels. Rub with extra-virgin olive oil and all seasonings along with liquid smoke.
3. Close the lid and flip the SmartSwitch to AIRFRY/STOVETOP. Select BAKE & ROAST, set temperature to 330°F, and set time to 50 minutes (unit will need to preheat for 5 minutes, so set an external timer if desired). Press START/STOP to begin cooking.
4. When the unit is preheated and the time reaches 45 minutes, place the roast on the tray. Close the lid to begin cooking.
5. After 25 minutes, open the lid and turn the roast over with silicone-tipped tongs to ensure even cooking. Close the lid to continue cooking.
6. Check for doneness using a meat thermometer and serve sprinkled with sliced jalapeños. Enjoy!

Gourmet Meatloaf (Bake&Roast)

Prep Time: 15 minutes, Cook Time: 25 minutes, Serves: 4

cooking spray   14-ounce lean ground beef   1 garlic clove, minced
1 chorizo sausage, chopped finely   Salt and black pepper, to taste   2 tbsps. olive oil
1 small onion, chopped 3 tbsps. breadcrumbs
2 tbsps. fresh mushrooms, sliced thinly

1. Push in the legs on the Crisper Tray, then place the tray in the bottom of the pot. Spray a baking pan with cooking spray.
2. Mix all the ingredients in a large bowl except mushrooms.
3. Place the beef mixture in the pan and smooth the surface with the back of spatula.
4. Top with mushroom slices and press into the meatloaf gently. Drizzle evenly with oil.
5. Close the lid and flip the SmartSwitch to AIRFRY/STOVETOP. Select BAKE & ROAST, set temperature to 390°F, and set time to 30 minutes (unit will need to preheat for 5 minutes, so set an external timer if desired). Press START/STOP to begin cooking.
6. When the unit is preheated and the time reaches 25 minutes, place the pan on the tray. Close the lid to begin cooking.
7. Cut into desires size wedges to serve.

Classic Moroccan Beef in Lettuce Cups (Slow Cook)

Prep Time: 21 minutes, Cook Time: 8 hours, Serves: 10

3 pounds (1.4 kg) grass-fed beef sirloin roast   1 cup grated carrot   ½ cup pomegranate seeds
1 (14-ounce / 397-g) BPA-free can no-salt-added   ¼ cup tomato paste   ½ cup beef stock
diced tomatoes, undrained   4 garlic cloves, cut into slivers
20 butter lettuce leaves   4 radishes, thinly sliced   1 tsp. ground cumin   1 tsp. ground cinnamon

1. Before getting started, be sure to remove the crisper tray.
2. Use a fork to poke holes in the sirloin roast and insert the slivers of garlic. Place the roast into the bottom of the pot.
3. Mix the beef stock, tomatoes, tomato paste, cumin, and cinnamon until well blended in a medium bowl. Pour the mixture over the roast.
4. Close the lid and flip the SmartSwitch to AIRFRY/STOVETOP. Select SLOW COOK, set temperature to "Lo", and set time to 8 hours. Press START/STOP to begin cooking, until the beef is soft.
5. Remove the beef from the pot and use two forks to shred.
6. In a large serving bowl, mix the beef with about 1 cup of the liquid from the pot.
7. Serve the beef mixture with the remaining ingredients.

Buttered Filet Mignon (Bake&Roast)

Prep Time: 10 minutes, Cook Time: 14 minutes, Serves: 4

cooking spray   2 (6-ounces) filet mignon steaks   pepper, to taste
1 tbsp. butter, softened   Salt   and   black

1. Push in the legs on the Crisper Tray, then place the tray in the bottom of the pot. Spray the tray with cooking spray.
2. Rub the steak generously with salt and black pepper and coat with butter.
3. Close the lid and flip the SmartSwitch to AIRFRY/STOVETOP. Select BAKE & ROAST, set temperature to 390°F, and set time to 19 minutes (unit will need to preheat for 5 minutes, so set an external timer if desired). Press START/STOP to begin cooking.
4. When the unit is preheated and the time reaches 14 minutes, place the steaks on the tray. Close the lid to begin cooking.
5. After 7 minutes, open the lid and flip the steaks with silicone-tipped tongs to ensure even cooking. Close the lid to continue cooking.
6. Dish out the steaks and cut into desired size slices to serve.

Corned Beef (Sear/Sauté)

Prep Time: 15 minutes, Cook Time: 15 minutes, Serves: 4

1 (12-ounce / 340-g) can corned beef   1 tsp. vegetable oil   ¼ tsp. dried thyme
¼ onion, chopped   ¼   green   bell   pepper,   ¼ tsp. crushed red pepper flakes
chopped   Salt and pepper to taste
¼ cup water   2 tsps. tomato paste

1. Before getting started, be sure to remove the Crisper Tray from the pot.
2. Flip the SmartSwitch to AIRFRY/STOVETOP. Select SEAR/SAUTÉ, choose "3". Press START/STOP to begin cooking.
3. In the pot, heat the oil. Add the green pepper, onion, red pepper flakes and dried thyme and sauté for 7 minutes.
4. Reduce the heat from "3" to "Lo1" and toss in the tomato paste, salt and pepper. Simmer for 3 minutes.
5. Stir in the corned beef and water and simmer until all the liquid is absorbed. Serve warm.

Beef Ramen with Pepperoni (Sear/Sauté)

Prep Time: 10 minutes, Cook Time: 15 minutes, Serves: 6

1 pound (454 g) ground beef, or to taste

16 slices pepperoni, or to taste

1 (14½-ounce / 411-g) can diced tomatoes

2 (3-ounce / 85-g) packages beef-flavored ramen

noodles

1 cup shredded Mozzarella cheese

1 green bell peppers, cut into strips

1 cup water

1. Before getting started, be sure to remove the Crisper Tray from the pot.
2. Flip the SmartSwitch to AIRFRY/STOVETOP. Select SEAR/SAUTÉ, choose "Hi5". Press START/STOP to begin cooking.
3. In the pot, sear the beef and pepperoni slices for 7 minutes. Then place tomatoes, content of seasoning packet content from ramen noodles and water into the pot containing beef.
4. After breaking ramen noodles into half, put this to the beef mixture along with green bell pepper and sauté for 5 minutes or until that noodles are soft.
5. Turn off the heat before adding Mozzarella cheese. Allow it to melt down before serving.

Fried Spinach & Tri Tip (Sous Vide)

Prep Time: 5 minutes, Cook Time: 2 hours, Serves: 2

1-piece tri tip roast

Kosher salt and black pepper

2 tsps. garlic powder   2 tsps. canola oil

1 pack baby spinach

1. Before getting started, remove the crisper tray and add 12 cups of room-temperature water to the pot (reference the marking on the inside of the pot).
2. Close the lid and flip the SmartSwitch to AIRFRY/STOVETOP. Select SOUS VIDE, set temperature to 145°F, and set time to 2 hours.
3. Press START/STOP to begin preheating.(Time for preheating depends on the temperature of the water added.)
4. Season the steak with pepper, garlic powder and salt
5. Add the steak in a Sous Vide bag.
6. When preheating is complete and "ADD FOOD" will show on the display.
7. Open the lid and place bag in the water using the water displacement method. When just the bag's seal is above the water line, finish closing the bag, making sure no water gets inside. Keep the bag's seal just above the water line.
8. Close the lid.
9. When cooking is complete, remove the bag with steak from cooker.
10. Take a cast-iron skillet and place it over medium-high heat.
11. After 2 minutes, put 1 tsp. of canola oil in the skillet.
12. Add the spinach and toss well.
13. Pour the bag juices into the skillet and toss well. Keep cooking for 30 seconds.
14. Transfer to a serving platter and slice the steak against the grain, into ¼ inch pieces.
15. Transfer it to the platter with the spinach and serve!

CHAPTER 7:
LAMB RECIPES

Pesto Coated Rack of Lamb and Farfalle (Speedi Meals)

Prep: 15 minutes, Total Cook Time: 30 minutes, Steam: approx. 10 minutes, Cook: 20 minutes, Serves: 4

LEVEL 1 (BOTTOM OF POT)
8 ounces Farfalle pasta   ½ cup tomato sauce
1 cup fresh spinach   2 cups water
LEVEL 2 (TRAY)
½ bunch fresh mint   1 (1½-pounds) rack of lamb

1 garlic clove   ¼ cup extra-virgin olive oil
½ tbsp. honey   Salt and black pepper, to taste
TOPPINGS:
Mint sauce   Sour cream

1. Place all Level 1 ingredients in the pot and stir to combine.
2. Pull out the legs on the Crisper Tray, then place the tray in the elevated position in the pot.
3. Put the mint, garlic, oil, honey, salt, and black pepper in a blender and pulse until smooth to make pesto.
4. Coat the rack of lamb with this pesto on both sides and arrange on top of the tray.
5. Close the lid and flip the SmartSwitch to RAPID COOKER.
6. Select SPEEDI MEALS, set temperature to 350°F, and set time to 20 minutes. Press START/STOP to begin cooking (the unit will steam for approx. 10 minutes before crisping).
7. When cooking is complete, remove the rack from the tray. Cut the rack into individual chops. Then use silicone-tipped tongs to grab the center handle and remove the tray from the unit. Transfer the pasta and spinach to a bowl, then top with the chops and desired toppings.

Leg of Lamb with Smoked Paprika (Sous Vide)

Prep Time: 10 minutes, Cook Time: 10 hours 10 minutes, Serves: 6

3 pounds lamb leg, bones removed
2 garlic cloves   1 tsp. ground smoked paprika
2 tbsps. dried oregano   1 garlic clove, minced

2 tbsps. olive oil   Salt and pepper to taste
Juice of 1 lemon

1. Before getting started, remove the crisper tray and add 12 cups of room-temperature water to the pot (reference the marking on the inside of the pot).
2. Close the lid and flip the SmartSwitch to AIRFRY/STOVETOP. Select SOUS VIDE, set temperature to 165°F, and set time to 10 hours.
3. Press START/STOP to begin preheating.(Time for preheating depends on the temperature of the water added.)
4. Prepare the seasoning: whisk together the minced garlic, olive oil, smoked paprika, salt, pepper and oregano.
5. Spread the mixture evenly over the lamb.
6. Put the lamb in a Sous Vide bag.
7. When preheating is complete and "ADD FOOD" will show on the display.
8. Open the lid and place bag in the water using the water displacement method. When just the bag's seal is above the water line, finish closing the bag, making sure no water gets inside. Keep the bag's seal just above the water line.
9. Close the lid.
10. When the time is up, place the lamb under the preheated grill for 4-5 minutes just until it becomes crispy.
11. Slice the cooked lamb and serve it sprinkled with lemon juice.

Ginger Lamb (Sear/Sauté)

Prep Time: 15 minutes, Cook Time: 15 minutes, Serves: 4

1 pound (454 g) boneless leg of lamb, cut into ¼-inch-thick slices

4 peeled fresh ginger slices, each about the size of a quarter

4 scallions, cut into 3-inch-long pieces, then thinly sliced lengthwise

3 garlic cloves, minced

2 whole dried red chili peppers (optional)

3 tbsps. vegetable oil, divided

2 tbsps. Shaoxing rice wine

1 tbsp. dark soy sauce

2 tsps. cornstarch   1 tsp. sesame oil

Kosher salt

1. Stir together the dark soy, rice wine, garlic, cornstarch and sesame oil in a large bowl. Place the lamb to the marinade and toss to coat well. Marinate for about 10 minutes.
2. Before getting started, be sure to remove the Crisper Tray from the pot.
3. Flip the SmartSwitch to AIRFRY/STOVETOP. Select SEAR/SAUTÉ, choose "Hi5". Press START/STOP to begin cooking.
4. Heat the pot until a drop of water sizzles and evaporates on contact.
5. Add 2 tbsps. of vegetable oil and swirl to coat the base of the pot well. Season the oil with the ginger, chilies (if using) and a pinch of salt. Let the aromatics sizzle in the oil for 30 seconds, swirling slowly.
6. Lift half the lamb from the marinade with tongs, shaking slightly to let the excess drip off. Reserve the marinade. Sear in the pot for about 2 to 3 minutes. Gently flip to sear on the other side for another 1 to 2 minutes. Sauté by tossing and flipping around in the pot immediately for 1 more minute. Transfer the lamb to a clean bowl. Pour in the remaining 1 tbsp. of vegetable oil and repeat this with the remaining lamb.
7. Take all of the lamb and the reserved marinade back to the pot and toss in the scallions. Sauté for another 1 minute, or until the lamb is cooked through and the marinade turns into a shiny sauce.
8. Transfer the lamb to a serving platter, discard the ginger and serve warm.

Lime Lamb and Chiles (Sear/Sauté)

Prep Time: 11 minutes, Cook Time: 5 minutes, Serves: 4

1 pound (454 g) lamb tenderloin, cut into 1-inch pieces, across the grain

1 medium onion, diced   2 or 3 Thai bird's eye chiles

Juice of 1 lime

4 scallions, cut into 1-inch pieces

2 garlic cloves, crushed and chopped

2 tbsps. cooking oil   1 tbsp. hot sesame oil

1 tbsp. ginger, crushed and chopped

1 tbsp. brown sugar   1 tbsp. fish sauce

1 tbsp. soy sauce   1 tbsp. cornstarch

1. Before getting started, be sure to remove the Crisper Tray from the pot.
2. Whisk together the lime juice, brown sugar, sesame oil and cornstarch in a small bowl. Keep aside.
3. Combine the soy sauce and fish sauce in a large bowl. Add the lamb and massage for about 1 minute.
4. Flip the SmartSwitch to AIRFRY/STOVETOP. Select SEAR/SAUTÉ, choose "Hi5". Press START/STOP to begin cooking.
5. Heat the cooking oi in the pot until it shimmers.
6. Add the garlic, ginger and lamb and sear for about 1 minute.
7. Place the bird's eye chiles and onion and sauté for about 1 minute.
8. Pour in the lime juice mixture and stir until a glaze is formed.
9. Sprinkle with the scallions and serve warm.

Cumin Lamb with Cilantro (Sear/Sauté)

Prep Time: 10 minutes, Cook Time: 5 minutes, Serves: 4

1 pound (454 g) boneless leg of lamb or shoulder, cut into 1-inch pieces
1 medium onion, diced
1 red bell pepper, cut into ½-inch pieces
½ cup cilantro, coarsely chopped
2 garlic cloves, crushed and chopped

2 tbsps. cooking oil   2 tbsps. soy sauce
1 tbsp. ginger, crushed and chopped
1 tbsp. ground cumin or cumin seeds
1 tbsp. cornstarch   1 tbsp. rice vinegar
1 tbsp. rice wine   ¼ tsp. kosher salt
½ tsp. ground black pepper

1. Before getting started, be sure to remove the Crisper Tray from the pot.
2. Flip the SmartSwitch to AIRFRY/STOVETOP. Select SEAR/SAUTÉ, choose "Hi5". Press START/STOP to begin cooking.
3. Heat the cooking oil in the pot until it shimmers.
4. Add the garlic, ginger and lamb and sear for about 1 minute.
5. Place the cumin, onion, salt and black pepper and sauté for about 1 minute.
6. Put the bell pepper and sauté for about 1 minute.
7. Pour the rice vinegar, rice wine, soy sauce and cornstarch and stir until a glaze is formed.
8. Sprinkle with the cilantro and serve warm.

Sweet Lamb and Cabbage (Sear/Sauté)

Prep Time: 7 minutes, Cook Time: 5 minutes, Serves: 5

1 pound (454 g) boneless leg of lamb or shoulder, cut into ¼-inch strips
1 cup Napa cabbage, shredded
1 medium onion, diced   ¼ cup rice vinegar
2 garlic cloves, crushed and chopped

2 tbsps. cooking oil   2 tbsps. soy sauce
2 tbsps. brown sugar   2 tbsps. cornstarch
1 tbsp. ginger, crushed and chopped
1 tsp. red pepper flakes

1. Before getting started, be sure to remove the Crisper Tray from the pot.
2. Whisk together the soy sauce, rice vinegar, brown sugar and cornstarch in a small bowl. Keep aside.
3. Flip the SmartSwitch to AIRFRY/STOVETOP. Select SEAR/SAUTÉ, choose "Hi5". Press START/STOP to begin cooking.
4. Heat the cooking oil in the pot until it shimmers.
5. Add the garlic, ginger, lamb, onion and red pepper flakes and sauté for about 2 minutes.
6. Pour in the soy sauce mixture and cabbage and stir until a glaze is formed.
7. Serve warm.

Lamb Loin Chops and Barley with Mushroom (Speedi Meals)

Prep: 20 minutes, Total Cook Time: 27 minutes, Steam: approx. 10 minutes, Cook: 17 minutes, Serves: 4

LEVEL 1 (BOTTOM OF POT)
1 cup cooked hulled barley
2 cups mushrooms, sliced
2 cups cheesy vegetable sauce   2 cups water
LEVEL 2 (TRAY)

8 (3½-ounces) bone-in lamb loin chops, trimmed
3 garlic cloves, crushed   1 tbsp. fresh lemon juice
1 tsp. olive oil   Salt and black pepper, to taste
TOPPINGS:
Salsa   Tzatziki

1. Place all Level 1 ingredients in the pot and stir to combine.
2. Pull out the legs on the Crisper Tray, then place the tray in the elevated position in the pot.
3. Mix the garlic, lemon juice, oil, salt, and black pepper in a large bowl.
4. Coat the chops generously with the herb mixture and arrange the chops on top of the tray.
5. Close the lid and flip the SmartSwitch to RAPID COOKER.
6. Select SPEEDI MEALS, set temperature to 375°F, and set time to 17 minutes. Press START/STOP to begin cooking (the unit will steam for approx. 10 minutes before crisping).
7. When cooking is complete, remove the chops from the tray. Then use silicone-lipped tongs to grab the center handle and remove the tray from the unit. Transfer the barley and mushroom to a bowl, then top with the chops and desired toppings.

Lamb Leg with Ginger and Leeks (Sear/Sauté)

Prep Time: 10 minutes, Cook Time: 15 minutes, Serves: 4

¾ pound (340 g) boneless leg of lamb, cut into 3 chunks, then thinly sliced across the grain
2 leeks, trimmed and thinly sliced
4 garlic cloves, finely minced
2 tbsps. vegetable oil
2 tbsps. Shaoxing rice wine

1 tbsp. peeled and finely minced fresh ginger
1 tbsp. dark soy sauce   1 tbsp. light soy sauce
1 to 2 tsps. sesame oil   2 tsps. cornstarch
1 tsp. honey   1 tsp. oyster sauce
½ tsp. ground Sichuan pepper corns
Kosher salt

1. Season the lamb lightly with 1 to 2 pinches of salt in a mixing bowl. Toss to coat and set aside for about 10 minutes.
2. Stir together the rice wine, light soy, dark soy, oyster sauce, honey, sesame oil, Sichuan pepper and cornstarch in a small bowl. Set aside.
3. Before getting started, be sure to remove the Crisper Tray from the pot.
4. Flip the SmartSwitch to AIRFRY/STOVETOP. Select SEAR/SAUTÉ, choose "Hi5". Press START/STOP to begin cooking.
5. Heat the pot until a drop of water sizzles and evaporates on contact.
6. Add the vegetable oil and swirl to coat the base of the pot well. Season the oil with the ginger and a pinch of salt. Let the ginger sizzle in the oil for about 10 seconds, swirling slowly.
7. Add the lamb and sear for about 1 to 2 minutes, then begin to sauté, gently tossing and flipping for 2 minutes more, or until no longer pink. Transfer the lamb to a clean bowl and set aside.
8. Add the garlic and leeks and sauté for about 1 to 2 minutes, or until the leeks are bright green and tender. Transfer to the lamb bowl.
9. Add the sauce mixture and simmer for about 3 to 4 minutes, until the sauce reduces by half and becomes glossy. Take the lamb and vegetables back to the pot and toss to combine with the sauce.
10. Transfer the dish to a platter and serve warm.

Garlic & Butter Lamb Chops (Sous Vide)

Prep Time: 10 minutes, Cook Time: 3 hours 10 minutes, Serves: 4

For the Lamb:
4 lamb chops   4 thyme sprigs
2 tbsps. olive oil   Salt and pepper to taste

For Searing:
2 tbsps. butter, melted   1 garlic clove, minced

1. Before getting started, remove the crisper tray and add 12 cups of room-temperature water to the pot (reference the marking on the inside of the pot).
2. Close the lid and flip the SmartSwitch to AIRFRY/STOVETOP. Select SOUS VIDE, set temperature to 145°F, and set time to 3 hours.
3. Press START/STOP to begin preheating.(Time for preheating depends on the temperature of the water added.)
4. Season the lamb shank with salt and pepper.
5. Put the lamb into the bag; add 2 tbsps. olive oil and 1 thyme sprig on each chop.
6. Put the lamb into a Sous Vide bag, add 2 tbsps. olive oil and 1 thyme sprig on each chop.
7. When preheating is complete and "ADD FOOD" will show on the display.
8. Open the lid and place bag in the water using the water displacement method. When just the bag's seal is above the water line, finish closing the bag, making sure no water gets inside. Keep the bag's seal just above the water line.
9. Close the lid.
10. When cooking is complete, combine the melted butter with the minced garlic, and coat each cooked chop with the butter-garlic mixture.
11. Sear each chop in the preheated cast iron skillet for 20 seconds on each side until golden.

Lamb Chops (Sous Vide)

Prep Time: 15 minutes, Cook Time: 2 hours 10 minutes, Serves: 2

2 lamb loin chops	Salt and pepper	1 tbsp. honey	1 tsp. extra-virgin olive oil
1 tsp. spice blend	4 prunes		

1. Before getting started, remove the crisper tray and add 12 cups of room-temperature water to the pot (reference the marking on the inside of the pot).
2. Close the lid and flip the SmartSwitch to AIRFRY/STOVETOP. Select SOUS VIDE, set temperature to 145°F, and set time to 2 hours.
3. Press START/STOP to begin preheating.(Time for preheating depends on the temperature of the water added.)
4. Season lamb chops thoroughly with salt and pepper. Rub the lamb chops with the spice blend.
5. In a Sous Vide bag, place the chops with prunes and honey.
6. When preheating is complete and "ADD FOOD" will show on the display.
7. Open the lid and place bag in the water using the water displacement method. When just the bag's seal is above the water line, finish closing the bag, making sure no water gets inside. Keep the bag's seal just above the water line.
8. Close the lid.
9. When cooking is complete, remove the lamb chops and save prunes and cooking liquid.
10. Take out the cooked lamb chops and pat them dry using a kitchen towel.
11. Place an iron skillet over medium heat for about 5 minutes.
12. Add the olive oil and the lamb chops and sear for 30 seconds per side.
13. Put on a serving plate and let it stand for 5 minutes.
14. Drizzle some of the cooking liquid from the bag over the chops and serve with the prunes.

Thyme Garlic Lamb Chops (Sous Vide)

Prep Time: 10 minutes, Cook Time: 2 hours, Serves: 4

8 lamb chops	2 tbsps. minced garlic	½ tbsp. lemon zest	Salt and pepper, to taste
4 sprigs fresh thyme	4 tbsps. olive oil		

1. Before getting started, remove the crisper tray and add 12 cups of room-temperature water to the pot (reference the marking on the inside of the pot).
2. Close the lid and flip the SmartSwitch to AIRFRY/STOVETOP. Select SOUS VIDE, set temperature to 145°F, and set time to 2 hours.
3. Press START/STOP to begin preheating.(Time for preheating depends on the temperature of the water added.)
4. Generously season lamb chops with salt and pepper.
5. In a Sous Vide bag, place the lamb chops along with garlic, thyme, olive oil, and lemon zest.
6. When preheating is complete and "ADD FOOD" will show on the display.
7. Open the lid and place bag in the water using the water displacement method. When just the bag's seal is above the water line, finish closing the bag, making sure no water gets inside. Keep the bag's seal just above the water line.
8. Close the lid.
9. When cooking is complete, remove the bag from a cooker.
10. Pat the lamb dry and place aside.
11. Heat some oil in a skillet. Sear the chops for 2 minutes per side, or use a torch to create a beautiful crust.
12. Serve warm.

CHAPTER 8:
POULTRY RECIPES

Chinese Chicken Drumsticks with Pasta (Speedi Meals)

Prep: 20 minutes, Total Cook Time: 30-35 minutes, Steam: approx. 10-15 minutes, Cook: 20 minutes, Serves: 4

LEVEL 1 (BOTTOM OF POT)
8 ounces penne pasta
1 (15 ounces) canned alfredo sauce
1 cup frozen cauliflower florets
1¼ cups water or stock

LEVEL 2 (TRAY)
4 (6-ounces) chicken drumsticks

1 cup corn flour   1 tbsp. oyster sauce
1 tsp. light soy sauce   ½ tsp. sesame oil
1 tsp. Chinese five spice powder
Salt and white pepper, as required

TOPPINGS:
Fresh herbs   Salsa
Guacamole   Sour cream

1. Place all Level 1 ingredients in the pot and stir to combine.
2. Pull out the legs on the Crisper Tray, then place the tray in the elevated position in the pot.
3. Mix the sauces, oil, five spice powder, salt, and black pepper in a bowl.
4. Rub the chicken drumsticks with marinade and refrigerate for about 30 minutes.
5. Arrange the drumsticks on top of the tray.
6. Close the lid and flip the SmartSwitch to RAPID COOKER.
7. Select SPEEDI MEALS, set temperature to 390°F, and set time to 20 minutes. Press START/STOP to begin cooking (the unit will steam for approx. 10 to 15 minutes before crisping).
8. When cooking is complete, remove the chicken drumsticks from the tray. Then use silicone-tipped tongs to grab the center handle and remove the tray from the unit. Transfer the pasta and cauliflower to a bowl, then top with the chicken drumsticks and desired toppings.

Nutty Chicken Tenders with Quinoa Meal (Speedi Meals)

Prep: 10 minutes, Total Cook Time: 25 minutes, Steam: approx. 10 minutes, Cook: 15 minutes, Serves: 4

LEVEL 1 (BOTTOM OF POT)
1 cup quinoa, rinsed   1 cup frozen peas
1 cup frozen broccoli florets
1 tsp. herb seasoning   1 cup water or stock
Salt and black pepper, to taste

LEVEL 2 (TRAY)
1 pound (454 g) chicken tenders

1 tsp. kosher salt   1 tsp. black pepper
½ tsp. smoked paprika   ¼ cup coarse mustard
2 tbsps. honey   1   cup   finely   crushed
pecans

TOPPINGS:
Salsa   Sour cream

1. Place all Level 1 ingredients in the pot and stir to combine.
2. Pull out the legs on the Crisper Tray, then place the tray in the elevated position in the pot.
3. Place the chicken in a large bowl. Sprinkle with the salt, pepper, and paprika. Toss until the chicken is coated with the spices. Add the mustard and honey and toss until the chicken is coated.
4. Put the pecans on a plate. Working with one piece of chicken at a time, roll the chicken in the pecans until both sides are coated. Lightly brush off any loose pecans. Place the chicken on top of the tray.
5. Close the lid and flip the SmartSwitch to RAPID COOKER.
6. Select SPEEDI MEALS, set temperature to 390°F, and set time to 15 minutes. Press START/STOP to begin cooking (the unit will steam for approx. 10 minutes before crisping).
7. When cooking is complete, remove the chicken from the tray. Then use silicone-tipped tongs to grab the center handle and remove the tray from the unit. Transfer the quinoa and vegetables to a bowl, then top with the chicken and desired toppings

Crisp Paprika Chicken Drumsticks (Steam&Crisp)

Prep: 5 minutes, Total Cook Time: 24 minutes, Steam: approx. 4 minutes, Cook: 20 minutes, Serves: 2

½ cup water, for steaming
1 tsp. packed brown sugar
½ tsp. dry mustard   ½ tsp. salt
Pinch pepper

2 tsps. paprika
1 tsp. garlic powder

4 (5-ounce / 142-g) chicken drumsticks, trimmed
1 tsp. vegetable oil
1 scallion, green part only, sliced thin on bias

1. Pour ½ cup water into the pot. Pull out the legs on the Crisper Tray, then place the tray in the elevated position in the pot.
2. Combine paprika, sugar, garlic powder, mustard, salt, and pepper in a bowl. Pat drumsticks dry with paper towels. Using metal skewer, poke 10 to 15 holes in skin of each drumstick. Rub with oil and sprinkle evenly with spice mixture. Arrange drumsticks on the tray, spaced evenly apart, alternating ends.
3. Close the lid and flip the SmartSwitch to Rapid Cooker. Select STEAM & CRISP, set temperature to 425°F, and set time to 20 minutes. Press START/STOP to begin cooking (the unit will steam for approx. 4 minutes before crisping).
4. With 10 minutes remaining, open the lid and flip the drumsticks with tongs. Close the lid to continue cooking.
5. Transfer chicken to serving platter, tent loosely with aluminum foil, and let rest for 5 minutes. Sprinkle with scallion and serve.

Chicken Manchurian (Steam&Crisp)

Prep: 10 minutes, Total Cook Time: 19 minutes, Steam: approx. 4 minutes, Cook: 15 minutes, Serves: 2

½ cup water, for steaming
1 pound (454 g) boneless, skinless chicken breasts, cut into 1-inch pieces
¼ cup ketchup
1 tbsp. tomato-based chili sauce, such as Heinz
1 tbsp. soy sauce   1 tbsp. rice vinegar

2 tsps. vegetable oil
1 tsp. hot sauce, such as Tabasco
½ tsp. garlic powder   ¼ tsp. cayenne pepper
2 scallions, thinly sliced
Cooked white rice, for serving

1. Pour ½ cup water into the pot. Pull out the legs on the Crisper Tray, then place the tray in the elevated position in the pot.
2. In a bowl, combine the chicken, ketchup, chili sauce, soy sauce, vinegar, oil, hot sauce, garlic powder, cayenne, and three-quarters of the scallions and toss until evenly coated.
3. Scrape the chicken and sauce into a metal cake pan and place the pan on the tray.
4. Close the lid and flip the SmartSwitch to Rapid Cooker. Select STEAM & CRISP, set temperature to 375°F, and set time to 15 minutes. Press START/STOP to begin cooking (the unit will steam for approx. 4 minutes before crisping).
5. With 7 minutes remaining, open the lid and toss the chicken with tongs. Close the lid to continue cooking.
6. When cooking is complete, use tongs to remove the pan from the tray. Spoon the chicken and sauce over rice and top with the remaining scallions. Serve immediately.

Ginger Chicken Thighs (Steam&Crisp)

Prep: 10 minutes, Total Cook Time: 19 minutes, Steam: approx. 4 minutes, Cook: 15 minutes, Serves: 4

½ cup water, for steaming
¼ cup julienned peeled fresh ginger
2 tbsps. vegetable oil   1 tbsp. honey
1 tbsp. soy sauce   1 tbsp. ketchup
1 tsp. garam masala   1 tsp. ground turmeric

¼ tsp. kosher salt   ½ tsp. cayenne pepper
Vegetable oil spray
1 pound (454 g) boneless, skinless chicken thighs, cut crosswise into thirds
¼ cup chopped fresh cilantro, for garnish

1. In a small bowl, combine the ginger, oil, honey, soy sauce, ketchup, garam masala, turmeric, salt, and cayenne. Whisk until well combined.
2. Place the chicken in a resealable plastic bag and pour the marinade over. Seal the bag and massage to cover all of the chicken with the marinade. Marinate at room temperature for 30 minutes or in the refrigerator for up to 24 hours.
3. Pour ½ cup water into the pot. Pull out the legs on the Crisper Tray, then place the tray in the elevated position in the pot. Spray the tray with vegetable oil spray
4. Add the chicken and as much of the marinade and julienned ginger as possible to the tray.
5. Close the lid and flip the SmartSwitch to Rapid Cooker. Select STEAM & CRISP, set temperature to 375°F, and set time to 15 minutes. Press START/STOP to begin cooking (the unit will steam for approx. 4 minutes before crisping).
6. With 7 minutes remaining, open the lid and toss the chicken with tongs. Close the lid to continue cooking.
7. When cooking is complete, use tongs to remove the chicken from the tray. Serve garnished with cilantro.

French Chicken, Mushroom and Wild Rice Stew (Slow Cook)

Prep Time: 14 minutes, Cook Time: 8 hours, Serves: 9

10 boneless, skinless chicken thighs, cut into 2-inch pieces
2 (14-ounce / 397-g) BPA-free cans diced tomatoes, undrained
3 large carrots, sliced   2 leeks, chopped
8 cups vegetable broth

2 cups sliced cremini mushrooms
1 cup wild rice, rinsed and drained
½ cup sliced ripe olives   3 garlic cloves, minced
2 tsp. dried herbes de Provence

1. Before getting started, be sure to remove the crisper tray.
2. Mix all the ingredients in the bottom of the pot.
3. Close the lid and flip the SmartSwitch to AIRFRY/STOVETOP. Select SLOW COOK, set temperature to "Lo", and set time to 8 hours. Press START/STOP to begin cooking, until the chicken is cooked to 165ºF and the wild rice is soft.
4. Serve warm.

Kadai Chicken with Yogurt (Sear/Sauté)

Prep Time: 10 minutes, Cook Time: 5 minutes, Serves: 4

1 pound (454 g) boneless chicken thighs, cut into 1-inch pieces
1 medium onion, cut into 1-inch pieces
1 medium carrot, roll-cut into ½-inch pieces
2 chiles, sliced into ¼-inch circles (no need to core or seed them)

½ cup whole-milk Greek yogurt
2 garlic cloves, crushed and chopped
2 tbsps. ghee
1 tbsp. ginger, crushed and chopped
1 tsp. cumin   1 tsp. ground coriander
1 tsp. paprika

1. Before getting started, be sure to remove the Crisper Tray from the pot.
2. Flip the SmartSwitch to AIRFRY/STOVETOP. Select SEAR/SAUTÉ, choose "Hi5". Press START/STOP to begin cooking.
3. Heat the ghee in the pot until it shimmers.
4. Add the garlic, ginger, carrot and chicken and sear for about 1 minute.
5. Place the onion, cumin, coriander and paprika and sauté for about 1 minute.
6. Then put the sliced chiles and sauté for about 1 minute.
7. Turn off the heat and stir the yogurt into the pot. Serve hot.

Garlic Kimchi Chicken and Cabbage (Sear/Sauté)

Prep Time: 8 minutes, Cook Time: 5 minutes, Serves: 4

1 pound (454 g) ground chicken
1 cup chopped kimchi
2 heads baby bok choy, leaves separated
2 garlic cloves, crushed and chopped
2 tbsps. cooking oil   2 tbsps. sesame seeds

1 tbsp. ginger, crushed and chopped
1 tbsp. fish sauce   1 tbsp. gochujang
1 tbsp. toasted sesame oil

1. Before getting started, be sure to remove the Crisper Tray from the pot.
2. Flip the SmartSwitch to AIRFRY/STOVETOP. Select SEAR/SAUTÉ, choose "Hi5". Press START/STOP to begin cooking.
3. Heat the cooking oil in the pot until it shimmers.
4. Add the garlic, ginger, and chicken and sear for about 2 minutes.
5. Put the kimchi, bok choy, gochujang and fish sauce and sauté for about 1 minute.
6. Pour in the sesame oil and sesame seeds and toss.
7. Serve hot.

Ginger Marmalade Chicken (Sous Vide)

Prep Time: 7 minutes, Cook Time: 3 hours 10 minutes, Serves: 4

2 lbs. bone-in skin-on chicken   4 tbsps. marmalade   2 tbsps. minced ginger   Salt and pepper

1. Before getting started, remove the crisper tray and add 12 cups of room-temperature water to the pot (reference the marking on the inside of the pot).
2. Close the lid and flip the SmartSwitch to AIRFRY/STOVETOP. Select SOUS VIDE, set temperature to 165°F, and set time to 3 hours.
3. Press START/STOP to begin preheating.(Time for preheating depends on the temperature of the water added.)
4. Season the chicken with salt and pepper.
5. In a Sous Vide bag, combine the chicken with remaining ingredients.
6. When preheating is complete and "ADD FOOD" will show on the display.

7. Open the lid and place bag in the water using the water displacement method. When just the bag's seal is above the water line, finish closing the bag, making sure no water gets inside. Keep the bag's seal just above the water line.
8. Close the lid.
9. When cooking is complete, remove the bag with chicken from cooker.
10. Transfer the cooked chicken to a baking dish.
11. Heat the broiler to a temperature of 500°F.
12. Arrange a rack, making sure it is 20 cm away from the heat source.
13. Place the baking dish to the broiler and broil for 10 minutes until crispy.
14. Remove and serve!

Ginger Duck Breast (Sous Vide)

Prep Time: 20 minutes, Cook Time: 1 hour 30 minutes, Serves: 2

2 boneless duck breasts   Kosher salt and pepper   2 garlic cloves, thinly sliced
1-inch fresh ginger, peeled, sliced thinly   1½ tsps. sesame oil

1. Before getting started, remove the crisper tray and add 12 cups of room-temperature water to the pot (reference the marking on the inside of the pot).
2. Close the lid and flip the SmartSwitch to AIRFRY/STOVETOP. Select SOUS VIDE, set temperature to 165°F, and set time to 1 hour 30 minutes.
3. Press START/STOP to begin preheating.(Time for preheating depends on the temperature of the water added.)
4. Season the duck breasts with pepper and salt.
5. In a Sous Vide bag, combine the duck breasts with ginger, sesame oil and garlic. Shake gently to coat the duck breasts.
6. When preheating is complete and "ADD FOOD" will show on the display.
7. Open the lid and place bag in the water using the water displacement method. When just the bag's seal is above the water line, finish closing the bag, making sure no water gets inside. Keep the bag's seal just above the water line.
8. Close the lid.
9. When cooking is complete, remove the duck and discard the garlic, ginger and cooking liquid.
10. Place the duck breast in a cold, non-stick skillet and put it over a high heat.
11. Cook the breast with the skin side down for about 30 seconds, flip, and cook for another 30 seconds.
12. Then place the breasts on a cutting board to rest for 5 minutes.
13. Slice the breasts and serve with your desired side dishes.

Chicken Saltimbocca (Sous Vide)

Prep Time: 15 minutes, Cook Time: 1 hour 30 minutes, Serves: 4

4 small chicken breasts, boneless, skinless   Freshly ground black pepper
8 sage leaves   1 tbsp. extra-virgin olive oil
4 pieces of thinly sliced prosciutto   2 oz. grated provolone

1. Before getting started, remove the crisper tray and add 12 cups of room-temperature water to the pot (reference the marking on the inside of the pot).
2. Close the lid and flip the SmartSwitch to AIRFRY/STOVETOP. Select SOUS VIDE, set temperature to 165°F, and set time to 1 hour 30 minutes.
3. Press START/STOP to begin preheating.(Time for preheating depends on the temperature of the water added.)
4. Transfer the chicken breast to a very clean flat surface and season with pepper and salt.
5. Top each of the chicken breast with sage leaves and 1 slice of prosciutto.
6. In a Sous Vide bag, place the chicken breasts.
7. When preheating is complete and "ADD FOOD" will show on the display.
8. Open the lid and place bag in the water using the water displacement method. When just the bag's seal is above the water line, finish closing the bag, making sure no water gets inside. Keep the bag's seal just above the water line.
9. Close the lid.
10. When cooking is complete, remove the chicken from the bag and pat dry.
11. Add some oil in a large skillet over a medium-high heat.
12. Put the chicken and prosciutto and sear for 1 minute.
13. Give the chicken pieces a flip and top each of the pieces with 1 tbsp. of provolone.
14. Cover the skillet with lid and cook for 30 seconds to allow the cheese to melt.
15. Add the chicken on a serving platter and garnish with sage leaves.
16. Serve!

CHAPTER 9:
SNACK RECIPES

Cod Nuggets (Steam&Crisp)

Prep: 15 minutes, Total Cook Time: 16 minutes, Steam: approx. 4 minutes, Cook: 12 minutes, Serves: 4

½ cup water, for steaming

1 cup all-purpose flour

2 eggs   ¾ cup breadcrumbs

1 pound cod, cut into 1x2½-inch strips

A pinch of salt   2 tbsps. olive oil

1. Pour ½ cup water into the pot. Pull out the legs on the Crisper Tray, then place the tray in the elevated position in the pot.
2. Place flour in a shallow dish and whisk the eggs in a second dish.
3. Place breadcrumbs, salt, and olive oil in a third shallow dish.
4. Coat the cod strips evenly in flour and dip in the eggs.
5. Roll into the breadcrumbs evenly and arrange the nuggets on the tray.
6. Close the lid and flip the SmartSwitch to Rapid Cooker. Select STEAM & CRISP, set temperature to 450°F, and set time to 12 minutes. Press START/STOP to begin cooking (the unit will steam for approx. 4 minutes before crisping).
7. With 6 minutes remaining, open the lid and flip the nuggets with tongs. Close the lid to continue cooking.
8. When cooking is complete, use tongs to remove the nuggets from the tray and serve warm.

Honey Sriracha Chicken Wings (Steam&Crisp)

Prep: 5 minutes, Total Cook Time: 29 minutes, Steam: approx. 4 minutes, Cook: 25 minutes, Serves: 4

½ cup water, for steaming

1 tbsp. Sriracha hot sauce

1 tbsp. honey   1 garlic clove, minced

½ tsp. kosher salt

8 chicken wings and drumettes

1. Pour ½ cup water into the pot. Push in the legs on the Crisper Tray, then place the tray in the bottom position in the pot.
2. In a large bowl, whisk together the Sriracha hot sauce, honey, minced garlic, and kosher salt, then add the chicken and toss to coat. Transfer the wings to the tray.
3. Close the lid and flip the SmartSwitch to Rapid Cooker. Select STEAM & CRISP, set temperature to 450°F, and set time to 25 minutes. Press START/STOP to begin cooking (the unit will steam for approx. 4 minutes before crisping).
4. With 10 minutes remaining, open the lid and flip the wings with tongs. Close the lid to continue cooking.
5. When cooking is complete, remove the wings and allow to cool on a wire rack for 10 minutes before serving.

Bacon-Wrapped Dates (Air Fry)

Prep Time: 10 minutes, Cook Time: 7 minutes, Serves: 6

12 dates, pitted   Cooking spray
6 slices high-quality bacon, cut in half

1. Push in the legs on the Crisper Tray, then place the tray in the bottom of the pot. Spray the tray with cooking spray.
2. Wrap each date with half a bacon slice and secure with a toothpick.
3. Close the lid and flip the SmartSwitch to AIRFRY/STOVETOP. Select AIRFRY, set temperature to 360°F, and set time to 12 minutes (unit will need to preheat for 5 minutes, so set an external timer if desired). Press START/STOP to begin cooking.
4. When the unit is preheated and the time reaches 7 minutes, place the bacon-wrapped dates on the tray. Close the lid to begin cooking, until the bacon is crispy.
5. When cooking is complete, remove the dates and allow to cool on a wire rack for 5 minutes before serving.

Crispy Mozzarella Sticks (Air Fry)

Prep Time: 5 minutes, Cook Time: 8 minutes, Serves: 4 to 8

1 egg   1 tbsp. water   8 Mozzarella string cheese "sticks"
8 eggroll wraps

1. Push in the legs on the Crisper Tray, then place the tray in the bottom of the pot. Spray the tray with cooking spray.
2. Beat together egg and water in a small bowl.
3. Lay out eggroll wraps and moisten edges with egg wash.
4. Place one piece of string cheese on each wrap near one end.
5. Fold in sides of eggroll wrap over ends of cheese, and then roll up.
6. Brush outside of wrap with egg wash and press gently to seal well.
7. Close the lid and flip the SmartSwitch to AIRFRY/STOVETOP. Select AIRFRY, set temperature to 375°F, and set time to 13 minutes (unit will need to preheat for 5 minutes, so set an external timer if desired). Press START/STOP to begin cooking.
8. When the unit is preheated and the time reaches 8 minutes, place the sticks on the tray. Close the lid to begin cooking.
9. After 4 minutes, open the lid and toss the sticks with silicone-tipped tongs to ensure even cooking. Close the lid to continue cooking.
10. When cooking is complete, serve immediately.

Cajun Zucchini Chips (Air Fry)

Prep Time: 5 minutes, Cook Time: 18 minutes, Serves: 4

2 large zucchini, cut into ⅛-inch-thick slices
2 tsps. Cajun seasoning   Cooking spray

1. Push in the legs on the Crisper Tray, then place the tray in the bottom of the pot. Spray the tray with cooking spray.
2. Put the zucchini slices in a medium bowl and spray them generously with cooking spray.
3. Sprinkle the Cajun seasoning over the zucchini and stir to make sure they are evenly coated with oil and seasoning.
4. Close the lid and flip the SmartSwitch to AIRFRY/STOVETOP. Select AIRFRY, set temperature to 390°F, and set time to 23 minutes (unit will need to preheat for 5 minutes, so set an external timer if desired). Press START/STOP to begin cooking.
5. When the unit is preheated and the time reaches 18 minutes, place the slices on the tray. Close the lid to begin cooking.
6. After 8 minutes, open the lid and flip the slices over with silicone-tipped tongs to ensure even cooking. Close the lid to continue cooking.
7. When cooking is complete, serve immediately.

Cheesy Apple Roll-Ups (Air Fry)

Prep Time: 5 minutes, Cook Time: 6 minutes, Makes: 8 roll-ups

cooking spray   ½ small apple, chopped
8 slices whole wheat sandwich bread   2 tbsps. butter, melted
4 ounces (113 g) Colby Jack cheese, grated

1. Push in the legs on the Crisper Tray, then place the tray in the bottom of the pot. Spray the tray with cooking spray.
2. Remove the crusts from the bread and flatten the slices with a rolling pin. Don't be gentle. Press hard so that bread will be very thin.
3. Top bread slices with cheese and chopped apple, dividing the ingredients evenly.
4. Roll up each slice tightly and secure each with one or two toothpicks.
5. Brush outside of rolls with melted butter.
6. Close the lid and flip the SmartSwitch to AIRFRY/STOVETOP. Select AIRFRY, set temperature to 390°F, and set time to 11 minutes (unit will need to preheat for 5 minutes, so set an external timer if desired). Press START/STOP to begin cooking.
7. When the unit is preheated and the time reaches 6 minutes, place the roll-ups on the tray. Close the lid to begin cooking, until outside is crisp and nicely browned.
8. Serve hot.

Sweet and Spicy Carrot Sticks (Air Fry)

Prep Time: 10 minutes, Cook Time: 12 minutes, Serves: 2

cooking spray
1 large carrot, peeled and cut into sticks
1 tbsp. fresh rosemary, chopped finely
1 tbsp. olive oil   2 tsps. sugar

¼ tsp. cayenne pepper
Salt and black pepper, to taste

1. Push in the legs on the Crisper Tray, then place the tray in the bottom of the pot. Spray the tray with cooking spray.
2. Mix carrot with all other ingredients in a bowl until well combined.
3. Close the lid and flip the SmartSwitch to AIRFRY/STOVETOP. Select AIRFRY, set temperature to 390°F, and set time to 17 minutes (unit will need to preheat for 5 minutes, so set an external timer if desired). Press START/STOP to begin cooking.
4. When the unit is preheated and the time reaches 12 minutes, place the carrot sticks on the tray. Close the lid to begin cooking.
5. After 6 minutes, open the lid and toss the carrot sticks with silicone-tipped tongs to ensure even cooking. Close the lid to continue cooking.
6. When cooking is complete, serve warm.

Rosemary Baked Cashews (Bake&Roast)

Prep Time: 5 minutes, Cook Time: 5 minutes, Makes: 2 cups

2 sprigs of fresh rosemary (1 chopped and 1 whole)
1 tsp. olive oil   1 tsp. kosher salt

½ tsp. honey   Cooking spray
2 cups roasted and unsalted whole cashews

1. Push in the legs on the Crisper Tray, then place the tray in the bottom of the pot. Spray the tray with cooking spray.
2. In a medium bowl, whisk together the chopped rosemary, olive oil, kosher salt, and honey. Set aside.
3. Close the lid and flip the SmartSwitch to AIRFRY/STOVETOP. Select BAKE & ROAST, set temperature to 300°F, and set time to 10 minutes (unit will need to preheat for 5 minutes, so set an external timer if desired). Press START/STOP to begin cooking.
4. When the unit is preheated and the time reaches 5 minutes, place the cashews and the whole rosemary sprig on the tray. Close the lid to begin cooking.
5. When cooking is complete, remove the cashews and rosemary to a bowl, then discard the rosemary and add the cashews to the olive oil mixture, tossing to coat.
6. Allow to cool for 15 minutes before serving.

Veggie Shrimp Toast (Bake&Roast)

Prep Time: 15 minutes, Cook Time: 6 minutes, Serves: 4

cooking spray
8 large raw shrimp, peeled and finely chopped
1 egg white   2 garlic cloves, minced
3 tbsps. minced red bell pepper
1 medium celery stalk, minced

2 tbsps. cornstarch
¼ tsp. Chinese five-spice powder
3 slices firm thin-sliced no-sodium whole-wheat bread

1. Push in the legs on the Crisper Tray, then place the tray in the bottom of the pot. Spray the tray with cooking spray.
2. In a small bowl, stir together the shrimp, egg white, garlic, red bell pepper, celery, cornstarch, and five-spice powder. Top each slice of bread with one-third of the shrimp mixture, spreading it evenly to the edges. With a sharp knife, cut each slice of bread into 4 strips.
3. Close the lid and flip the SmartSwitch to AIRFRY/STOVETOP. Select BAKE & ROAST, set temperature to 350°F, and set time to 11 minutes (unit will need to preheat for 5 minutes, so set an external timer if desired). Press START/STOP to begin cooking.
4. When the unit is preheated and the time reaches 6 minutes, place the shrimp toasts on the tray. Close the lid to begin cooking.
5. When cooking is complete, serve hot.

Warm Spiced Apple Chips (Dehydrate)

Prep Time: 10 minutes, Cook Time: 8 hours, Serves: 2

1 apple, peeled, cored and thinly sliced
1 tbsp. coconut sugar   ½ tsp. ground cinnamon
Pinch of ground cardamom

Pinch of ground ginger
Pinch of salt

1. Mix together all the ingredients in a bowl until well combined.
2. Spread the apple slices on dehydrator rack.
3. Push in the legs on the Crisper Tray, then place the tray in the bottom position in the pot. Put the rack with apple slices on the tray.
4. Close the lid and flip the SmartSwitch to AIRFRY/STOVETOP. Select DEHYDRATE, set temperature to 135°F, and set time to 8 hours. Press START/STOP to begin cooking.
5. Remove the apple slices from the cooker, serve immediately.

CHAPTER 10:

DESSERT RECIPES

Pumpkin Pudding (Steam&Bake)

Prep: 10 minutes, Total Cook Time: 30 minutes, Steam: approx. 20 minutes, Cook: 10 minutes, Serves: 4

1 cup water, for steaming	cooking spray
3 cups pumpkin purée	3 tbsps. honey
1 tbsp. ginger	1 tbsp. cinnamon
1 tsp. clove	1 tsp. nutmeg
1 cup full-fat cream	2 eggs
1 cup sugar	

1. Pour 1 cup water into the pot. Push in the legs on the Crisper Tray, then place the tray in the bottom position in the pot. Spray a 8-inch round baking pan with cooking spray.
2. In a bowl, stir all the ingredients together to combine.
3. Scrape the mixture into the the prepared baking pan and transfer the pan on the tray.
4. Close the lid and flip the SmartSwitch to Rapid Cooker. Select STEAM & BAKE, set temperature to 390°F, and set time to 10 minutes. Press START/STOP to begin cooking (the unit will steam for approx. 20 minutes before baking).
5. Serve warm.

Avocado Walnut Bread (Steam&Bake)

Prep: 5 minutes, Total Cook Time: 45 minutes, Steam: approx. 20 minutes, Cook: 25 minutes, Serves: 6

2 cups water, for steaming	2 tbsps. (¾ oz.) Toasted walnuts, chopped roughly
¾ cup (3 oz.) almond flour, white	1 tsp. cinnamon ground
¼ tsp. baking soda	½ tsp. kosher salt 2 tbsps. olive oil
2 ripe avocados, cored, peeled and mashed	½ cup granulated swerve
2 large eggs, beaten	1 tsp. vanilla extract

1. Pour 2 cups water into the pot. Push in the legs on the Crisper Tray, then place the tray in the bottom position in the pot. Line a 6-inch baking pan with parchment paper.
2. Mix almond flour, salt, baking soda, and cinnamon in a bowl.
3. Whisk eggs with avocado mash, yogurt, swerve, oil, and vanilla in a bowl.
4. Stir in the almond flour mixture and mix until well combined.
5. Pour the batter evenly into the pan and top with the walnuts. Then place the pan on the tray.
6. Close the lid and flip the SmartSwitch to Rapid Cooker. Select STEAM & BAKE, set temperature to 315°F, and set time to 25 minutes. Press START/STOP to begin cooking (the unit will steam for approx. 20 minutes before baking).
7. Dish out in a platter and cut into slices to serve.

Black Forest Pies (Steam&Bake)

Prep: 10 minutes, Total Cook Time: 30 minutes, Steam: approx. 15 minutes, Cook: 15 minutes, Serves: 6

1 cup water, for steaming   cooking spray
3 tbsps. milk or dark chocolate chips
2 tbsps. thick, hot fudge sauce
2 tbsps. chopped dried cherries

1 (10-by-15-inch) sheet frozen puff pastry, thawed
1 egg white, beaten   2 tbsps. coconut sugar
½ tsp. cinnamon

1. Pour 1 cup water into the pot. Push in the legs on the Crisper Tray, then place the tray in the bottom position in the pot. Spray the tray with cooking spray.
2. In a small bowl, combine the chocolate chips, fudge sauce, and dried cherries.
3. Roll out the puff pastry on a floured surface. Cut into 6 squares with a sharp knife.
4. Divide the chocolate chip mixture into the center of each puff pastry square. Fold the squares in half to make triangles. Firmly press the edges with the tines of a fork to seal.
5. Brush the triangles on all sides sparingly with the beaten egg white. Sprinkle the tops with sugar and cinnamon. Transfer the triangles on the tray.
6. Close the lid and flip the SmartSwitch to Rapid Cooker. Select STEAM & BAKE, set temperature to 350°F, and set time to 15 minutes. Press START/STOP to begin cooking (the unit will steam for approx. 15 minutes before baking).
7. When cooking is complete, allow to cool for at least 20 minutes before serving.

Blueberry Cake (Steam&Bake)

Prep: 10 minutes, Total Cook Time: 40 minutes, Steam: approx. 20 minutes, Cook: 20 minutes, Serves: 6

2 cups water, for steaming
cooking spray   3 eggs
1 cup almond flour
1 stick butter, room temperature

⅓ cup blueberries
1½ tsps. baking powder
½ cup sour cream   ⅔ cup swerve
2 tsps. vanilla

1. Pour 2 cups water into the pot. Push in the legs on the Crisper Tray, then place the tray in the bottom position in the pot. Spray a 8-inch round baking pan with cooking spray.
2. Mix all the ingredients in a bowl except blueberries.
3. Pour the batter in the baking pan and fold in the blueberries.
4. Mix well and transfer the pan on the tray.
5. Close the lid and flip the SmartSwitch to Rapid Cooker. Select STEAM & BAKE, set temperature to 350°F, and set time to 20 minutes. Press START/STOP to begin cooking (the unit will steam for approx. 20 minutes before baking).
6. When cooking is complete, carefully remove the pan and allow to cool for 5 minutes. Cut into slices to serve.

Chocolaty Squares (Steam&Bake)

Prep: 15 minutes, Total Cook Time: 40 minutes, Steam: approx. 20 minutes, Cook: 20 minutes, Serves: 4

1 cup water, for steaming   cooking spray   1¼-ounce brown sugar
2-ounce cold butter   3-ounce self-rising flour   ⅛ cup honey
½ tbsp. milk   2-ounce chocolate, chopped

1. Pour 1 cup water into the pot. Push in the legs on the Crisper Tray, then place the tray in the bottom position in the pot. Spray a tin with cooking spray.
2. Mix butter, brown sugar, flour and honey and beat till smooth.
3. Stir in the chocolate and milk and pour the mixture into a tin, then place the tin on the tray.
4. Close the lid and flip the SmartSwitch to Rapid Cooker. Select STEAM & BAKE, set temperature to 315°F, and set time to 20 minutes. Press START/STOP to begin cooking (the unit will steam for approx. 20 minutes before baking).
5. Dish out and cut into desired squares to serve.

Simple Pineapple Sticks (Air Fry)

Prep Time: 5 minutes, Cook Time: 10 minutes, Serves: 4

cooking spray   ½ fresh pineapple, cut into sticks
¼ cup desiccated coconut

1. Push in the legs on the Crisper Tray, then place the tray in the bottom of the pot. Spray the tray with cooking spray.
2. Coat the pineapple sticks in the desiccated coconut.
3. Close the lid and flip the SmartSwitch to AIRFRY/STOVETOP. Select AIRFRY, set temperature to 350°F, and set time to 15 minutes (unit will need to preheat for 5 minutes, so set an external timer if desired). Press START/STOP to begin cooking.
4. When the unit is preheated and the time reaches 10 minutes, place the pineapple sticks on the tray. Close the lid to begin cooking.
5. After 5 minutes, open the lid and flip the pineapple sticks with silicone-tipped tongs to ensure even cooking. Close the lid to continue cooking.
6. When cooking is complete, serve immediately.

Peach Brown Betty with Cranberries (Slow Cook)

Prep Time: 20 minutes, Cook Time: 6 hours, Serves: 10

⅓ cup melted coconut oil   ⅓ cup coconut sugar
8 ripe peaches, peeled and cut into chunks   3 tbsps. honey
3 cups cubed whole-wheat bread   2 tbsps. freshly squeezed lemon juice
1½ cups whole-wheat bread crumbs   ¼ tsp. ground cardamom
1 cup dried cranberries

1. Before getting started, be sure to remove the crisper tray.
2. Mix the peaches, dried cranberries, lemon juice, and honey in the bottom of the pot.
3. In a large bowl, mix the bread crumbs, bread cubes, coconut sugar, and cardamom. Pour the melted coconut oil over all and toss to coat well.
4. Place the bread mixture on the fruit in the pot.
5. Close the lid and flip the SmartSwitch to AIRFRY/STOVETOP. Select SLOW COOK, set temperature to "Lo", and set time to 6 hours. Press START/STOP to begin cooking, until the fruit is bubbling and the topping is browned.
6. Serve warm.

Honey-Roasted Pears (Bake&Roast)

Prep Time: 5 minutes, Cook Time: 20 minutes, Serves: 4

cooking spray
2 large Bosc pears, halved and deseeded
3 tbsps. honey   1 tbsp. unsalted butter

½ tsp. ground cinnamon   ¼ cup walnuts, chopped
¼ cup part skim low-fat ricotta cheese, divided

1. Push in the legs on the Crisper Tray, then place the tray in the bottom of the pot. Spray a 8-inch round baking pan with cooking spray.
2. Place the pears, cut side up on the baking pan.
3. In a small microwave-safe bowl, melt the honey, butter, and cinnamon. Brush this mixture over the cut sides of the pears.
4. Pour 3 tbsps. of water around the pears in the pan.
5. Close the lid and flip the SmartSwitch to AIRFRY/STOVETOP. Select BAKE & ROAST, set temperature to 350°F, and set time to 25 minutes (unit will need to preheat for 5 minutes, so set an external timer if desired). Press START/STOP to begin cooking.
6. When the unit is preheated and the time reaches 20 minutes, place the pan on the tray. Close the lid to begin cooking, until tender, basting once with the liquid in the pan.
7. Carefully remove the pears from the pan and place on a serving plate. Drizzle each with some liquid from the pan, sprinkle the walnuts on top, and serve with a spoonful of ricotta cheese.

Curry Peaches, Pears, and Plums (Bake&Roast)

Prep Time: 5 minutes, Cook Time: 8 minutes, Serves: 6 to 8

2 peaches   2 firm pears
2 plums   2 tbsps. melted butter

1 tbsp. honey   2 to 3 tsps. curry powder

1. Push in the legs on the Crisper Tray, then place the tray in the bottom of the pot.
2. Cut the peaches in half, remove the pits, and cut each half in half again. Cut the pears in half, core them, and remove the stem. Cut each half in half again. Do the same with the plums.
3. Spread a large sheet of heavy-duty foil on the work surface. Arrange the fruit on the foil and drizzle with the butter and honey. Sprinkle with the curry powder.
4. Wrap the fruit in the foil, making sure to leave some air space in the packet.
5. Close the lid and flip the SmartSwitch to AIRFRY/STOVETOP. Select BAKE & ROAST, set temperature to 325°F, and set time to 13 minutes (unit will need to preheat for 5 minutes, so set an external timer if desired). Press START/STOP to begin cooking.
6. When the unit is preheated and the time reaches 8 minutes, place the foil package on the tray. Close the lid to begin cooking.
7. When cooking is complete, serve hot.

Spongy Cinnamon Donuts (Bake&Roast)

Prep Time: 10 minutes, Cook Time: 8 minutes, Serves: 8

cooking spray

For the Donuts:

2¼ cups plain flour

1½ tsps. baking powder

2 large egg yolks   2 tbsps. butter, melted

Salt, to taste   ½ cup sugar

½ cup sour cream

For the Cinnamon Sugar:

⅓ cup caster sugar   1 tsp. cinnamon

1. Push in the legs on the Crisper Tray, then place the tray in the bottom of the pot. Spray the tray with cooking spray.
2. Sift together flour, baking powder and salt in a large bowl.
3. Add sugar and cold butter and mix until a coarse crumb is formed.
4. Stir in the egg yolks, ½ of the sour cream and ⅓ of the flour mixture and mix until a dough is formed.
5. Add remaining sour cream and ⅓ of the flour mixture and mix until well combined. Stir in the remaining flour mixture and combine well.
6. Roll the dough into ½ inch thickness onto a floured surface and cut into donuts with a donut cutter. Coat butter on both sides of the donuts.
7. Close the lid and flip the SmartSwitch to AIRFRY/STOVETOP. Select BAKE & ROAST, set temperature to 350°F, and set time to 13 minutes (unit will need to preheat for 5 minutes, so set an external timer if desired). Press START/STOP to begin cooking.
8. When the unit is preheated and the time reaches 8 minutes, place the donuts on the tray. Close the lid to begin cooking, until golden.
9. When cooking is complete, sprinkle with cinnamon sugar to serve.

Pear and Apple Crisp (Bake&Roast)

Prep Time: 10 minutes, Cook Time: 20 minutes, Serves: 6

cooking spray   1 cup flour

½ pound (227 g) apples, cored and chopped

½ pound (227 g) pears, cored and chopped

1 cup sugar   1 tbsp. butter

1 tsp. ground cinnamon   ¼ tsp. ground cloves

1 tsp. vanilla extract   ¼ cup chopped walnuts

Whipped cream, for serving

1. Push in the legs on the Crisper Tray, then place the tray in the bottom of the pot. Spray a 8-inch round baking pan with cooking spray.
2. Place the apples and pears into the baking pan.
3. Combine the rest of the ingredients, minus the walnuts and the whipped cream, until a coarse, crumbly texture is achieved.
4. Pour the mixture over the fruits and spread it evenly. Top with the chopped walnuts.
5. Close the lid and flip the SmartSwitch to AIRFRY/STOVETOP. Select BAKE & ROAST, set temperature to 350°F, and set time to 25 minutes (unit will need to preheat for 5 minutes, so set an external timer if desired). Press START/STOP to begin cooking.
6. When the unit is preheated and the time reaches 20 minutes, place the pan on the tray. Close the lid to begin cooking, until the top turns golden brown.
7. Serve at room temperature with whipped cream.

APPENDIX 1: 14-DAY MEAL PLAN

Meal Plan	Breakfast	Lunch	Dinner	Snack/Dessert
Day-1	Zucchini Fritters (Steam&Crisp)	Tasty Mahi Mahi Meal (Speedi Meals)	Lamb Leg with Ginger and Leeks (Sear/Sauté)	Crispy Mozzarella Sticks (Air Fry)
Day-2	Parmesan Sausage Egg Muffins (Steam&Bake)	Avocado Buttered Flank Steak with Pea Rice (Speedi Meals)	Pasta Vegetables Stew (Slow Cook)	Chocolaty Squares (Steam&Bake)
Day-3	Egg Veggie Frittata (Steam&Bake)	Lime Lamb and Chiles (Sear/Sauté)	Pork Hoagies (Sous Vide)	Honey-Roasted Pears (Bake&Roast)
Day-4	Kale and Quinoa Egg Casserole (Slow Cook)	Chicken Manchurian (Steam&Crisp)	Amazing Salmon Fillets (Steam&Crisp)	Cheesy Apple Roll-Ups (Air Fry)
Day-5	Toasties and Sausage in Egg Pond (Steam&Crisp)	Sesame Pork and Carrot (Sear/Sauté)	French Chicken, Mushroom and Wild Rice Stew (Slow Cook)	Avocado Walnut Bread (Steam&Bake)
Day-6	Tasty Toasts (Bake&Roast)	Italian Eggplant Parmesan (Slow Cook)	Crumbed Golden Filet Mignon (Air Fry)	Honey Sriracha Chicken Wings (Steam&Crisp)
Day-7	Zucchini Fritters (Steam&Crisp)	Spicy Orange Shrimp (Air Fry)	Sweet and Sour Pork and Pineapple (Sear/Sauté)	Pumpkin Pudding (Steam&Bake)
Day-8	Gold Avocado (Air Fry)	Holiday Spicy Beef Roast (Bake&Roast)	Cheesy Sausage Balls and Bulgur Wheat (Speedi Meals)	Rosemary Baked Cashews (Bake&Roast)

Day-9	Bacon and Hot Dogs Omelet (Steam&Bake)	Kadai Chicken with Yogurt (Sear/Sauté)	Almond Asparagus (Bake&Roast)	Peach Brown Betty with Cranberries (Slow Cook)
Day-10	Flavorful Bacon Cups (Steam&Bake)	Lamb Loin Chops and Barley with Mushroom (Speedi Meals)	White Fish and Spinach Risotto (Slow Cook)	Cajun Zucchini Chips (Air Fry)
Day-11	Cream Bread (Steam&Bake)	Thyme Garlic Lamb Chops (Sous Vide)	Classic Moroccan Beef in Lettuce Cups (Slow Cook)	Curry Peaches, Pears, and Plums (Bake&Roast)
Day-12	Honey Carrot Cake Oatmeal (Slow Cook)	Sweet and Spicy Parsnips (Steam&Crisp)	Cumin Lamb with Cilantro (Sear/ Sauté)	V e g g i e Shrimp Toast (Bake&Roast)
Day-13	Simple Scotch Eggs (Bake&Roast)	Garlic Squid (Sous Vide)	Thai Pork and Mushroom with Peanut Sauce (Slow Cook)	Blueberry Cake (Steam&Bake)
Day-14	Bacon and Hot Dogs Omelet (Steam&Bake)	Beef Ramen with Pepperoni (Sear/ Sauté)	Herbed Potatoes (Steam&Crisp)	Bacon-Wrapped Dates (Air Fry)

APPENDIX 2: NINJA SPEEDI SF301 TIMETABLE

Steam & Crisp Chart

INGREDIENT	AMOUNT	PREPARATION	WATER	ORIENTATION	TEMP	COOK TIME
VEGETABLES						
Acorn squash	1	Cut in half, placed face down	½ cup	Bottom	390°F	15 mins
Beets	2½ lbs	Cut in 1-in pieces	½ cup	Bottom	400°F	30–35 mins
Broccoli	1 head	Whole, stem removed	½ cup	Bottom	400°F	10-15 mins
Brussels sprouts	2 lbs	Cut in half, ends trimmed	½ cup	Bottom	450°F	15–20 mins
Carrots	1 lb	Cut in 1-in pieces	½ cup	Bottom	400°F	20-25 mins
Cauliflower	1 head	Whole, stems removed	½ cup	Bottom	425°F	20-25 mins
Parsnip	2½ lbs	Cut in 1-in pieces	½ cup	Bottom	400°F	30–35 mins
Potatoes, russet	2 lbs	Cut in 1-in wedges	½ cup	Bottom	450°F	25–30 mins
	2 lbs	Hand-cut fries, soaked 30 mins in cold water then patted dry	½ cup	Bottom	450°F	30–35 mins
	4	Whole (medium), poked several times with a fork	1 cup	Bottom	400°F	30–35 mins
		Whole (large), poked several times with a fork	1 cup	Bottom	400°F	40–48 mins
	2½ lbs	Cut in 1-in pieces	½ cup	Bottom	450°F	30–35 mins
Spaghetti squash	1 small squash	Cut in half, deseeded, punctured with fork about 10 times	2 cups	Bottom	375°F	25–30 mins
Sweet potatoes	2½ lbs	Cut in 1-in pieces	½ cup	Bottom	450°F	20–25 mins
POULTRY						
Whole chicken	4½–5 lbs	Trussed	1 cup	Bottom	400°F	40–50 mins
Turkey drumstricks	2 lbs	None	1 cup	Bottom	400°F	32–38 mins
Turkey breast	1 (3–5 lbs)	None	1 cup	Bottom	365°F	45–55 mins
Chicken breasts (boneless)	4 breasts, 6–8 oz each	Brush with oil	½ cup	Elevated	390°F	15–20 mins
Chicken breasts (bone in, skin on)	4 breasts, ¾–1½ lbs	Brush with oil	½ cup	Elevated	375°F	20–25 mins
Chicken thighs (bone in)	4 thighs, 6–10 oz each	Brush with oil	½ cup	Elevated	400°F	20–25 mins
Chicken thighs (boneless)	6 thighs, 4–8 oz each	Brush with oil	½ cup	Elevated	375°F	15–18 mins
Chicken drumsticks	2 lbs	Brush with oil	½ cup	Elevated	425°F	20–25 mins
Hand-breaded chicken breasts	4 breasts, 6 oz each		½ cup	Elevated	385°F	18–20 mins
Chicken wings	2 lbs		½ cup	Bottom	450°F	20–25 mins
PORK						
Pork tenderloins	2 (1 lb each)	None	1 cup	Elevated	375°F	25–30 mins
Pork loin	1 (2 lbs)	None	1 cup	Elevated	365°F	35–40 mins
Spiral ham, bone in	1 (3 lbs)	None	1 cup	Elevated	325°F	45–50 mins
Pork chops, boneless	4 chops, 6–8 oz each	None	½ cup	Bottom	375°F	15-20 mins
Pork chops (bone in, thick cut)	2 chops, 10–12 oz each		½ cup	Bottom	375°F	25–30 mins

*NOTE: Crisper tray position varies, as specified in chart. Steam will take approximately 4–8 minutes to build.

Steam & Crisp Chart

INGREDIENT	AMOUNT	PREPARATION	WATER	ORIENTATION	TEMP	COOK TIME
FISH						
Cod	4 fillets, 6 oz each		½ cup	Elevated	450°F	9–12 mins
Salmon	4 fillets, 6 oz each		¼ cup	Elevated	450°F	7–10 mins
Scallops	1 lb (approx. 21 pieces)		¼ cup	Elevated	400°F	4–6 mins
BEEF						
Roast beef	2–3 lbs	None	1 cup	Bottom	360°F	45 mins for medium rare
Tenderloin	2–3 lbs	None	1 cup	Bottom	365°F	25–30 mins for medium rare
FROZEN CHICKEN						
Chicken Breasts, Boneless, Skinless	4 breasts, 4–6 oz each	As desired	½ cup	Elevated	390°F	20–25 mins
Chicken Thighs, Boneless, Skinless	6 thighs, 4–8 oz each	As desired	½ cup	Elevated	375°F	15–20 mins
Chicken Thighs, Bone-in Skin on	4 thighs, 8–10 oz each	As desired	½ cup	Elevated	400°F	20–25 mins
Pre-Breaded Chicken Breasts	3–4 breasts, 10–16 oz each	As desired	½ cup	Elevated	375°F	10–15 mins
Chicken Wings	2 lbs	As desired	½ cup	Bottom	450°F	25–30 mins
FROZEN BEEF						
NY Strip Steak	2 steaks, 10–14 oz each	2 tbsp canola oil, salt, pepper	¾ cup	Bottom	400°F	22–28 mins
FROZEN FISH						
Salmon	4 fillets, 6 oz each		½ cup	Elevated	450°F	11–15 mins
Shrimp	18 shrimp, 1 lb		½ cup	Bottom	450°F	2–5 mins
Cod	4 fillets, 6 oz each		½ cup	Elevated	450°F	10–15 mins
Lobster tails	4		½ cup	Elevated	450°F	5–7 mins
FROZEN PORK						
Pork tenderloins	2 (1 lb each)	None	1½ cups	Bottom	365°F	30–35 mins
Pork loin	1 (2 lbs)	None	None	Bottom	360°F	37–40 mins
Pork chops, boneless	4, 6–8 oz each		½ cup	Elevated	375°F	15–20 mins
Pork Chops, bone-in, thick cut	2, 10–12 oz each		¾ cup	Elevated	365°F	23–28 mins
Italian sausages	6 uncooked		½ cup	Elevated	375°F	10–12 mins
FROZEN PREPARED FOODS						
Dumplings/Pot stickers	16 oz bag		½ cup	Bottom	400°F	12–16 mins
Ravioli	25 oz bag		½ cup	Bottom	385°F	12–16 mins
Eggrolls	10 oz pkg		½ cup	Bottom	375°F	15–20 mins

*NOTE: Crisper tray position varies, as specified in chart. Steam will take approximately 4–8 minutes to build.

Air Fry Chart for the Crisper Tray, bottom position

INGREDIENT	AMOUNT	PREPARATION	OIL	TEMP	COOK TIME
VEGETABLES					
Asparagus	1 bunch	Cut in half, trim stems	2 tsp	390°F	8–10 mins
Beets	6 small or 4 large (about 2 lbs)	Whole	None	390°F	45–60 mins
Bell peppers	4 peppers	Whole	None	400°F	25–30 mins
Broccoli	1 head	Cut in 1–2-inch florets	1 Tbsp	390°F	10–13 mins
Brussels sprouts	1 lb	Cut in half, remove stems	1 Tbsp	390°F	15–18 mins
Butternut squash	1–1½ lbs	Cut in 1–2-inch pieces	1 Tbsp	390°F	20–25 mins
Carrots	1 lb	Peeled, cut in ½-inch pieces	1 Tbsp	390°F	14–16 mins
Cauliflower	1 head	Cut in 1–2-inch florets	2 Tbsp	390°F	15–20 mins
Corn on the cob	4 ears, cut in half	Whole, remove husks	1 Tbsp	390°F	12–15 mins
Green beans	1 bag (12 oz)	Trimmed	1 Tbsp	390°F	7–10 mins
Kale (for chips)	6 cups, packed	Tear in pieces, remove stems	None	300°F	8–11 mins
Mushrooms	8 oz	Rinse, cut in quarters	1 Tbsp	390°F	7–8 mins
Potatoes, russet	1½ lbs	Cut in 1-inch wedges	1 Tbsp	390°F	20–25 mins
	1 lb	Hand-cut fries, thin	½–3 Tbsp	390°F	20–25 mins
	1 lb	Hand-cut fries, soak 30 mins in cold water then pat dry	½–3 Tbsp	390°F	24–27 mins
	4 whole (6–8 oz)	Pierce with fork 3 times	None	390°F	35–40 mins
Potatoes, sweet	2 lbs	Cut in 1-inch chunks	1 Tbsp	390°F	15–20 mins
	4 whole (6–8 oz)	Pierce with fork 3 times	None	390°F	35–40 mins
Zucchini	1 lb	Cut in quarters lengthwise, then cut in 1-inch pieces	1 Tbsp	390°F	15–20 mins
POULTRY					
Chicken breasts	2 breasts (¾–1½ lbs each)	Bone in	Brushed with oil	375°F	25–35 mins
	2 breasts (½–¾ lb each)	Boneless	Brushed with oil	375°F	22–25 mins
Chicken thighs	4 thighs (6–10 oz each)	Bone in	Brushed with oil	390°F	22–28 mins
	4 thighs (4–8 oz each)	Boneless	Brushed with oil	390°F	18–22 mins
Chicken wings	2 lbs	Drumettes & flats	1 Tbsp	390°F	24–28 mins
Chicken, whole	1 chicken (4–6 lbs)	Trussed	Brushed with oil	375°F	55–75 mins
Chicken drumsticks	2 lbs	None	1 Tbsp	390°F	20–22 mins

*TIP When using Air Fry, add 5 minutes to the suggested cook time for the unit to preheat before you add ingredients.

Air Fry Chart for the Crisper Tray, bottom position

INGREDIENT	AMOUNT	PREPARATION	OIL	TEMP	COOK TIME
BEEF					
Burgers	4 quarter-pound patties, 80% lean	1-inch thick	None	375°F	10–12 mins
Steaks	2 steaks (8 oz each)	Whole	None	390°F	10–20 mins
PORK & LAMB					
Bacon	1 strip to 1 (16 oz) package	Lay strips evenly over the plate	None	330°F	13–16 mins (no preheat)
Pork chops	2 thick-cut, bone-in chops (10–12 oz each)	Bone in	Brushed with oil	375°F	15–17 mins
	4 boneless chops (6–8 oz each)	Boneless	Brushed with oil	375°F	15–18 mins
Pork tenderloins	2 tenderloins (1–1½ lbs each)	Whole	Brushed with oil	375°F	25–35 mins
Sausages	4 sausages	Whole	None	390°F	8–10 mins
FISH & SEAFOOD					
Crab cakes	2 cakes (6–8 oz each)	None	Brushed with oil	350°F	10–13 mins
Lobster tails	4 tails (3–4 oz each)	Whole	None	375°F	7–10 mins
Salmon fillets	2 fillets (4 oz each)	None	Brushed with oil	390°F	10–13 mins
Shrimp	16 jumbo	Raw, whole, peel, keep tails on	1 Tbsp	390°F	7–10 mins
FROZEN FOODS					
Chicken nuggets	1 box (12 oz)	None	None	390°F	11–13 mins
Fish fillets	1 box (6 fillets)	None	None	390°F	13–15 mins
Fish sticks	1 box (14.8 oz)	None	None	390°F	9–11 mins
French fries	1 lb	None	None	360°F	18–22 mins
	2 lbs	None	None	360°F	28–32 mins
Mozzarella sticks	1 box (11 oz)	None	None	375°F	6–9 mins
Pot stickers	1 bag (10 count)	None	Toss with 1 tsp oil	390°F	11–14 mins
Pizza Rolls	1 bag (20 oz, 40 count)	None	None	390°F	12–15 mins
Popcorn shrimp	1 box (16 oz)	None	None	390°F	8–10 mins
Tater Tots	1 lb	None	None	360°F	19–22 mins

*TIP When using Air Fry, add 5 minutes to the suggested cook time for the unit to preheat before you add ingredients.

Dehydrate Chart   for the Crisper Tray, bottom position

INGREDIENT	PREPARATION	TEMP	DEHYDRATE TIME
FRUITS & VEGETABLES			
Apple chips	Cut in ⅛-inch slices (remove core), rinse in lemon water, pat dry	135°F	7–8 hrs
Asparagus	Cut in 1-inch pieces, blanch	135°F	6–8 hrs
Bananas	Peel, cut in 3/8-inch slices	135°F	8–10 hrs
Beet chips	Peel, cut in ⅛-inch slices	135°F	7–8 hrs
Eggplant	Peel, cut in ¼-inch slices, blanch	135°F	6–8 hrs
Fresh herbs	Rinse, pat dry, remove stems	135°F	4–6 hrs
Ginger root	Cut in 3/8-inch slices	135°F	6 hrs
Mangoes	Peel, cut in 3/8-inch slices, remove pits	135°F	6–8 hrs
Mushrooms	Clean with soft brush (do not wash)	135°F	6–8 hrs
Pineapple	Peel, cut in 3/8–½-inch slices, core removed	135°F	6–8 hrs
Strawberries	Cut in half or in ½-inch slices	135°F	6–8 hrs
Tomatoes	Cut in 3/8-inch slices or grate; steam if planning to rehydrate	135°F	6–8 hrs
JERKY – MEAT, POULTRY, FISH			
Beef jerky	Cut in ¼-inch slices, marinate overnight	150°F	5–7 hrs
Chicken jerky	Cut in ¼-inch slices, marinate overnight	150°F	5–7 hrs
Turkey jerky	Cut in ¼-inch slices, marinate overnight	150°F	5–7 hrs
Salmon jerky	Cut in ¼-inch slices, marinate overnight	165°F	5–8 hrs

*TIP Most fruits and vegetables take between 6 and 8 hours (at 135°F) to dehydrate; meats take between 5 and 7 hours (at 150°F). The longer you dehydrate your ingredients, the crispier they will be.

Sous Vide Chart   Crisper Tray not used

INGREDIENT	AMOUNT	TEMP	COOK TIME
BEEF			
Boneless ribeye	2 steaks, 14 oz each, 1–2 inches thick	125°F Rare	1–5 hrs
Boneless ribeye	3 steaks, 14 oz each, 1–2 inches thick	130°F Medium Rare	1–5 hrs
		135°F Medium	1–5 hrs
Porterhouse	2 steaks, 14 oz each, 1–2 inches thick	145°F Medium Well	1–5 hrs
Filet mignon	4 steaks, 8 oz each, 1–2 inches thick	155°F Well Done	1–5 hrs
Flank	3 steaks, 12 oz each, 1–2 inches thick	125°F Rare	2–5 hrs
		130°F Medium Rare	2–5 hrs
		135°F Medium	2–5 hrs
Flat iron	2 steaks, 10 oz each, 1–2 inches thick	145°F Medium Well	2–5 hrs
		155°F Well Done	2–5 hrs
Beef brisket	3 lbs, 3–4 inches thick	145°F	24–48 hrs
PORK			
Boneless pork chops	5 chops, 6–8 oz each, 2½ inches thick	145°F	1–4 hrs
Bone-In pork chops	2 chops, 10–12 oz each, 2½ inches thick	145°F	1–4 hrs
Tenderloin	1 tenderloin, 1–1½ lbs, 2½ inches thick	145°F	1–4 hrs
Sausages	6 sausages, 2–3 oz each	165°F	2–5 hrs
Boneless pork shoulder	3 lbs, 3–4 inches thick	165°F	12–24 hrs
CHICKEN			
Chicken Breast	6 breasts, 6–8 oz each, 1–2 inches thick	165°F	1–3 hrs
Boneless Chicken Thighs	6 thighs, 4–6 oz each, 1–2 inches thick	165°F	1–3 hrs
Bone-In Chicken Thighs	4 thighs, 4–6 oz each, 1–2 inches thick	165°F	1½–4 hrs
Chicken Leg Quarters	2 quarters, 12–14 oz each, 1–2 inches thick	165°F	1½–4 hrs
Chicken Wings & Drummettes	2 lbs	165°F	1–3 hrs
Half Chicken	2½–3 lbs	165°F	2–3 hrs
SEAFOOD			
Whitefish (Cod, Haddock, Pollock)	2 portions, 6–10 oz each, 1–2 inches thick	130°F	1 hr–1½ hrs
Salmon	4 portions, 6–10 oz each, 1–2 inches thick	130°F	1 hr–1½ hrs
Shrimp	2 lbs	130°F	30 mins–2 hrs
VEGETABLES			
Asparagus	1–2 lbs	180°F	30 mins
Broccoli	1–1½ lbs	180°F	30 mins
Brussels Sprouts	1–2 lbs	180°F	45 mins
Carrots	1–1½ lbs	180°F	45 mins
Cauliflower	1–1½ lbs	180°F	30 mins
Green Beans	1–1½ lbs	180°F	30 mins
Squash	1–1½ lbs	185°F	1 hr
Sweet Potatoes	1–1½ lbs	185°F	1 hr
Potatoes	1–2 lbs	190°F	1 hr

*TIP Cook time is dependent on the weight as well as the thickness of food, so thicker cuts of meat will require longer cook times. If your ingredients are thicker than 2½ inches, add more time.

APPENDIX 3: RECIPES INDEX

D-K

Date

Bacon-Wrapped Dates (Air Fry)   56

Duck Breast

Ginger Duck Breast (Sous Vide)   53

Eggplant

Italian Eggplant Parmesan (Slow Cook)   21

Filet Mignon

Crumbed Golden Filet Mignon (Air Fry)   37
Buttered Filet Mignon (Bake&Roast)   40

Flank Steak

Avocado Buttered Flank Steak with Pea Rice (Speedi Meals)   36
Miso Marinated Steak and Spinach Pasta (Speedi Meals)   37

Haddock

Herbed Haddock (Bake&Roast)   26

Kale

Kale and Quinoa Egg Casserole (Slow Cook)   15

L-P

Lamb Chop

Garlic & Butter Lamb Chops (Sous Vide)   46
Thyme Garlic Lamb Chops (Sous Vide)   47

Lamb Leg

Ginger Lamb (Sear/Sauté)   44
Cumin Lamb with Cilantro (Sear/Sauté)   45
Lamb Leg with Ginger and Leeks (Sear/Sauté)   46
Sweet Lamb and Cabbage (Sear/Sauté)   45
Leg of Lamb with Smoked Paprika (Sous Vide)   43

Lamb Loin Chop

Lamb Loin Chops and Barley with Mushroom (Speedi Meals)   45
Lamb Chops (Sous Vide)   46

Lamb Rack

Pesto Coated Rack of Lamb and Farfalle (Speedi Meals)   43

Lamb Tenderloin

Lime Lamb and Chiles (Sear/Sauté)   44

Mahi Mahi

Tasty Mahi Mahi Meal (Speedi Meals)   23

Parsnip

Sweet and Spicy Parsnips (Steam&Crisp)   18

Peach

Curry Peaches, Pears, and Plums (Bake&Roast)   64
Peach Brown Betty with Cranberries (Slow Cook)   63

Pear

Honey-Roasted Pears (Bake&Roast)   64

Pineapple

Simple Pineapple Sticks (Air Fry)   63

Pork

Thai Pork with Basil (Sear/Sauté)   32
Pork and Brussels Sprouts with Oyster Sauce (Sear/Sauté) 34

Pork Belly

Five Spice Pork and Quinoa with Asparagus (Speedi Meals)   30

Pork Chop

Breaded Pork Chops and Cherry Tomato Pasta (Speedi Meals)   30
Cheese Crusted Chops (Air Fry)   31

Pork Loin Roast

Thai Pork and Mushroom with Peanut Sauce (Slow Cook) 32

Pork Porterhouse

Coffee-Chili Pork Porterhouse (Sous Vide)   31

Pork Sausage

Simple Scotch Eggs (Bake&Roast)   14

Pork Shoulder Chop

Pork Hoagies (Sous Vide)   33

Pork Tenderloin

Sweet and Sour Pork and Pineapple (Sear/Sauté) 33
Sesame Pork and Carrot (Sear/Sauté)   34

Printed in Great Britain
by Amazon

22081150R00046